S0-AAM-547

# GHASTLY GOOD TASTE

*By the Same Author*
*(with James Press)*
MOUNT ZION

*(with John Murray)*
FIRST AND LAST LOVES
SUMMONED BY BELLS
A RING OF BELLS
HIGH AND LOW
COLLECTED POEMS (Enlarged Edition)

# JOHN BETJEMAN

# Ghastly

# GOOD TASTE

## or, a depressing story of the rise and fall of English Architecture

*Why, child, the only hope thou hast*
*Lies in thy master's want of taste;*
*For shou'd his ling'ring stay in London*
*Improve your taste, you must be undone*

William Whitehead
*Poems on Several Occasions*, 1754

ANTHONY BLOND

First published by Chapman & Hall Ltd., 1933
Copyright 1933 John Betjeman

This edition © John Betjeman 1970

Anthony Blond Ltd.
56 Doughty Street, W.C.1

218 51156 6

DESIGNED BY SEBASTIAN CARTER

PRINTED IN GREAT BRITAIN BY

W & J MACKAY & CO LTD, CHATHAM

TO
PENELOPE CHETWODE

# Preface

The author is indebted to so many persons and friends for so much conversation and advice that he can but specify some whose direct influence and help make it possible for him to express particular gratitude. First, his host and hostess in Westmeath have caused this book to exist. Next, Mr Peter Fleetwood-Hesketh's brilliant drawing at the end of the book is far clearer and far more important than the text. Next, from de Cronin Hastings came much help, though not as much as in former times. Mr Frederick Etchells, F.R.I.B.A., kindly played Batty Langley to the author's Lord Ongley. Mr Arthur Waugh gave valuable assistance. The author acknowledges the interest of his father in looking over the proofs, for his advice, coupled with that of a friend of high position and peculiar appearance, did much to rid the text of some of its prejudices.

Mr E. W. Hamilton and Mr W. E. Levear, of Messrs Chapman & Hall, and Mr A. E. Doyle, of Gravesend, and Lady Mary St Clair Erskine, of Horsham, have been of great assistance over the format and typography. Finally, the author is indebted to Mr C. S. Lewis, of Oxford, whose jolly personality and encouragement to the author in his youth have remained an unfading memory for the author's declining years.

# Contents

# List of Illustrations

There is only one illustration, nine feet long, which pulls out at the back of the book and which was the result of the keen observation and subtle draughtsmanship of Mr Peter Fleetwood-Hesketh.

# *Introduction · An Aesthete's Apologia*

I wrote this book thirty-eight years ago. I was twenty-six, in love, and about to be married. When Anthony Blond said he would like to reprint it, I thought I had better read it, and he kindly sent me a copy. I am appalled by its sententiousness, arrogance and the sweeping generalisations in which it abounds. The best things about it are the fancy cover, which I designed myself from display types found in the capacious nineteenth-century premises of Stevens, Shanks & Sons, 89 Southwark Street, type founders. In their collection they discovered for me the little railway train and the founts which in descending order are Ultra Bodoni, Argentine, Bodoni, Rustic. I have an idea that the sans-serif outline capitals in which the word 'Illustration' is written, is a Grotesque. The black letter for 'Mr Fleetwood-Hesketh' is Westminster. The text of the book is in a modern face, because most books on architecture in the early thirties were printed in a sans-serif a long way after Gill, and to print a book of this size and to use an italic running commentary at the top of each right-hand page was hopelessly old-fashioned.

Display types were generally sans-serif and title-page and cover had to be pure and empty-looking, and nothing quite in the middle, so as to show that it was up to date.

The real point of the book was the Street of Taste, or the March of English Art down the Ages, specially drawn by Peter

Fleetwood-Hesketh, with traffic to match. This pull-out was also an old-fashioned thing to do, and the style of architectural caricature was deliberately based on Pugin's caricatures in his book *Contrasts* (1836). This pull-out was what caused people to buy the book, and looking back at it, I regard it as far less modish and much more balanced than the text. Mr Fleetwood-Hesketh has kindly continued the depressing theme up to 1970.

I thought it might be helpful to attempt an aesthetic auto-biography up to the date when this book was published. Most people who were small children when the 1914 war started and with an interest in buildings, will have had similar aesthetic experiences. I have thought it best to be extremely personal at the risk of seeming egotistic, because I can see no other way of explaining the state of mind which enabled me to dash out this book in something like a white-hot fury.

My own interest started in seeking out what was old. When the guide told me that this was the bed in which Queen Elizabeth slept, I believed him. When owners of country cottages in Suffolk told me their cottage was a thousand years old, I believed them too. I thought that this or that church was the smallest in England, and that secret passages ran under ruined monasteries, so that monks could get to the nearest convent without being seen. The older anything was the lovelier I thought it. I was quite uncritical, as are hundreds of thousands of my fellow citizens in the same happy state of childlike innocence about architecture.

The next stage of interest started at about the age of twelve. This was a preoccupation with the different styles of mediaeval parish churches. It goes with detective fiction, for it is great fun discovering a half-hidden Norman arch or a blocked-up squint or a banner-stave locker (whatever that may have been). Saxon was crude and rude and scarce, Norman was strong and bold like William the Conqueror and easy to recognise, because the arches were round. The next style, Early English, was the purest, because it was the beginning of Gothic, and things are always pure when they begin. The next style was the curvilinear and geometrical tracery and foliated capitals of Decorated, the middle style and generally regarded as the perfection of Gothic. For when things are in their middle they are perfect. After this came the debased but omnipresent Perpendicular style, which was to be found in all the churches I knew, particularly in those of Norfolk and Cornwall.

Uncritically in these days I loved every Tudor manor house and thatched cottage on a green and every timber-framed tile-hung farmhouse with brick chimney stacks. Doubtless many a church which I admired as the perfection of Gothic, that is to say, Decorated, was really Victorian, while most of the thatched and tile-hung houses and Tudor manor houses were Victorian too. I could not tell the fake from the genuine.

I think a sense of architecture in the round comes with puberty. It is then that one begins to appreciate proportion and shape and lines of construction. At my private school, Lynam's, at Oxford, I was lucky enough to be allowed to go off with friends bicycling in the limestone villages of Oxon., and also to visit the colleges in the University itself. By the time I had reached my public school at Marlborough in Wiltshire, the absence of limestone, the comparative paucity of parish churches within bicycling distance, the bare chalk downs, beechwoods, brick cottages and thatched barns, did not have the appeal of either Oxford and the Cotswolds, or the tall flint wool churches of Norfolk, or those granite and round-roofed boat-builders' jobs, the churches of Cornwall. Life was rougher, food was worse, and fears were greater.

Architecture was hardly mentioned at Marlborough and it was not until I was over sixteen that I became aware of it as part of the school surroundings. Then there were two influences working in contrary directions. There was that good, delightful and hospitable man Colonel Christopher Hughes, the art master. He treated us as adults and led us off on sketching expeditions to villages which were then remote, down chalky and flinty lanes rarely invaded by the motor car. Here we would sit in front of a thatched barn, a haystack or a row of summer elms and make a rough outline in pencil of what we saw, before applying the watercolour. 'Wet the whole surface for sky, apply cobalt and ultramarine but no prussian blue, and if you want a grey cloud add light red to the ultramarine while the surface is still wet. Now apply blotting paper or a handkerchief to get the patchy effect of clouds. The sky should be a deeper blue at the top, paling as it reaches the horizon.' When the paint dried the effect was indeed often quite remarkable. After that one painted the rest of the picture using a light yellow first where it was needed, either on its own or as a background to greens. 'Never use artificial greens, like green bice, but make your own out of combinations of yellow and blue.'

All this industry was accompanied by talk about anything except sex. Then there was tea in a cottage with Wiltshire lardy cake. I was never much good at watercolours. John Edward Bowle, the historian, was much the best, and won the Art Cup in 1924. He could paint the downs, big elm trees heavy with shadow and thatched cottages, worthy of an R.S.W. or even an R.A. These sketching expeditions taught me to appreciate the importance of the setting of a building, the shapes of trees, and the effects of light in different weathers, and at different times of day. I still secretly thought that if anyone had invented colour photography—and they had not invented it then—there would be no need for us to do watercolours. Constable and Arnesby Brown, my father's two favourite landscape artists, I thought had they known about colour photography, would have used the camera instead of going to all that trouble with oil paint. As for the pre-Raphaelites, obviously they would have used colour cameras.

Meanwhile there was an anti-art master and sketching movement in the school. This was headed by Ellis Waterhouse (now Professor of Fine Arts and Director of the Barber Institute, Birmingham) and Anthony Blunt (now Keeper of the Queen's Pictures and Director of the Courtauld Institute of Art). It was through them and Anthony's elder brother, Wilfred, that we art enthusiasts learned of the existence of the French Impressionists and particularly the painting of Cézanne, which Christopher Hughes thought little of. I do not think Ellis or Anthony ever drew or painted anything themselves, certainly they never went on Christopher Hughes's sketching expeditions. But they told us about Clive Bell and Significant Form and Roger Fry. They were much cleverer boys than the rest of us, and early became members of the sixth and of the entourage of 'Gussie', that is to say Mr G. N. Sargeaunt, a remote, distinguished figure, whom it was never my privilege to know. To Christopher Hughes these original and useful Marlborough aesthetes were pretentious. He did not think that they understood about perspective and technique, and he had anyhow little sympathy with Impressionism. He was at heart a pre-Raphaelite. His father was the Hughes of Ward & Hughes, stained-glass artists, and his father had trained him. His father died, aged 100, in the late 1940s. Meanwhile Anthony Blunt bought for us reproductions of Italian primitives and Renaissance painters, which we hung in our studies. These paintings made me realise I could never be an artist myself, I would never master the technique. I began to believe that English painting was provincial and not 'great'. The Italians and the French are the only good painters. This made Christopher Hughes defend the Dutch. We were much pleasurably torn by this aesthetic dispute. When I say 'we' I mean the aesthetes at Marlborough, for it was at that time a Philistine and hearty school, where games were worshipped and the O.T.C. was compulsory. The courage and influence of Anthony Blunt, and the continued tolerance and kindness of Christopher Hughes, and most important of all the formation of an Art Society gave us hope and happiness. The Art Society was inspired by two distinguished housemasters, Clifford Canning, later Headmaster of Canford, and George Turner, later Master of Marlborough, and finally

Headmaster of Charterhouse. They lent us their rooms, their books and their hospitality.

Hitherto architecture had been a pleasure only for the holidays. Holidays in London were the most rewarding. My father was fond of Georgian silver and furniture. I liked Georgian books for the smell of their cream-coloured paper, their wide margins, brownish black type and the use of the long $\int$ for *s*. I read, without fully understanding them, most of the poems in Dodsley's Miscellany. Part of the joy of this was that eighteenth-century poetry was not considered good by English Literature standards at school. It was thought artificial. Thereafter the artificial became my hobby. The more artificial it was the more I liked it. An uncle gave me a copy of Austin Dobson's 'Ballad of Beau Brocade', with illustrations by Hugh Thompson. Dobson seemed to me a better poet even than the eighteenth-century ones themselves.

> *Phyllida my Phyllida*
> *She dons her russet gown*
> *And runs to gather maydew*
> *Before the world is down.*

Goodness knows what gathering maydew was, I didn't question such beauty. In the Mound on which had stood a castle at Marlborough, Lady Hertford had in the eighteenth century caused a grotto to be built and a spiral path to ascend the mountain's brow. The grotto was used as a potato shed and kept locked. Through a wire grating I could just espy the felspar and shells with which its walls were adorned and, I delighted in the words of Stephen Duck, Lady Hertford's tame Wiltshire poet:

> *Calypso, thus attended by her train,*
> *With rural palaces adorns the plain.*

On sketching expeditions I now spurned the old cottages and sought out eighteenth-century buildings. The most beautiful I saw in the neighbourhood was Ramsbury Manor House, a more sophisticated version of Lady Hertford's dwelling at Marlborough. It stood in a landscaped park and could be seen from a bridge across a lake, a gravel drive curling elegantly up its front door. No words can express my longing to get inside this house, and to see its furniture and library. What the Louvre was to Anthony Blunt and the Parthenon to the boring master who taught us Greek, Ramsbury Manor was to me. I think the mystery of its winding drive gave me a respect for the system of hereditary landowning which I have never shaken off. Christopher Hughes understood this interest in eighteenth-century buildings, and sympathised with my inability to draw Ramsbury and Classical symmetry to my, or his, satisfaction. It also set him, and eventually the aesthetes, into discussing the merits and demerits of the Victorians. Christopher Hughes regarded Landseer as a ridiculous artist, and his picture 'Dignity and Impudence' of two dogs, as a debasement of art. Thenceforward with the natural contrariness of my nature, I became fascinated by Victorian art and architecture. I extended the fascination to poets, and read long epics like *Israel in Egypt* by Edwin Atherstone. I bought at second-hand bookshops Keepsakes and similar annuals with steel engravings and Byronic lyrics. I bought Victorian anthologies of poetry with wood engravings by Birket Foster and Pinwell. These could then be purchased for sixpence or a shilling and in mint condition. I read a paper to the Art Society ridiculing, while half admiring, Victorian poets and artists. Their architecture I thought then was not to be taken seriously, as it was purely imitative and rather vulgar.

Holidays were spent exploring churches. Those in London pleased me most as I had outgrown most parish churches of mediaeval date in East Anglia and Cornwall. All I wanted to see was the Renaissance. I visited every London church attributed to Wren and his successors. I read the criticisms of George Godwin Junior in *The Churches of London* (2 vols.), C. Tilt, 1839, and of James Elmes in *Metropolitan Improvements, or London in the 19th century*, London, Jones & Co., 1827. Through these books I learned architectural terms, Greek, Roman and Gothic, structural and detail. I also read every Edwardian book on architecture I could find. By the time I reached Oxford in 1925, I had become bored by Gothic, whether it was genuine or false. This may have been largely due to the still unforgivable technological terms people will use when describing mediaeval buildings—the wearisome footnotes and the anxiety not to be caught out by being wrong in an attribution or a date. The letters F.S.A after a name have always, since those days, caused me to shudder. I realise now that antiquaries have become more liberal in their opinions and that the new profession of architectural history has done what was hardly attempted in the 1920s, it has discriminated between the shoddy and the solid and it has even admitted the present century into its consideration. But in the late twenties and early thirties the heralds of that discrimination were few and little heard. At Oxford, where I could buy books from Blackwell's and had no conscience about running up bills which I hoped my father would eventually pay, I bought Professor Richardson's *Monumental Classic Architecture in Great Britain and Ireland*, Batsford, 1912. With its large sepia photographs, measured drawings, and informed text, it opened to me a world more exciting even than that of Hawksmoor and Vanburgh. I had never before heard of anyone admiring the British Museum for its architecture, or Somerset House or St George's Hall, Liverpool, or Waterloo Bridge, which was then still standing to Rennie's design. I started to look at the Romano-Greek and Banks by C. R. Cockerell and Euston Great Hall and Portico by P. C. Hardwick. The Professor became my hero, and has always remained so.

There were, of course, the officially approved books on officially approved architecture, that is to say Jacobean and early English Renaissance and the work of Lutyens and the gardens for early Lutyens houses laid out by Miss Jekyll. These, however, were less interesting to me than what could then be bought for five or ten shillings at the many suburban and provincial second-hand bookshops which then abounded. Here I found late eighteenth-century and early nineteenth-century books of designs for lodges, villas, and country mansions, illustrated with sepia and sometimes with coloured aquatints.

These gave me a vision of Georgian England which was utterly different from those seen in the big Batsford books or in the books of watercolours of different counties and towns published by A. and C. Black. It was a different England too from that so romantically illustrated in the drawings by F. L. Griggs in the 'Highways and Byeways' series published by Macmillan. These Georgian aquatinted books added to my respect for the landed proprietor, with his gate lodge, park, walled garden, pinetum, icehouse, library, saloon, home farm and spreading stables. I had already had a taste for this sort of thing when staying in the houses of Oxford friends. Nowhere though could the eighteenth-century country house as shown in the aquatint more perfectly be seen than in Ireland. Oxford friends of Anglo-Irish descent asked me to their castles, abbeys and halls in the quiet Midlands of Ireland. The leisurely train journey from Harcourt Street or Kingsbridge, the locked Church of Ireland church in a Gothic only one removed from the Gothick of Strawberry Hill, the winding avenue and sheet of water, the fine outward show and the inward damp splendour slightly dried by burning logs in some marble-surrounded hearth, made me think Ireland the most beautiful country in the world, and its inhabitants the most learned and poetical. Nor have I ever ceased to admire the Anglo-Irish race, which has produced so many great sailors, soldiers, revolutionaries and writers.

No one in the late twenties, however, with the hunger marches and the unemployed in England, could help regarding the sort of Ireland I venerated as anything but an escape. Many

of my Oxford friends, and it was at Oxford, rather than at
school or in later life, that I made the most, were actively engaged in politics, and of course most of my friends who were
aesthetes were Left-wing. In the General Strike, under the influence of Hugh Gaitskell, Lionel Perry and John Dugdale, all
of whom were interested in architecture and art, as well as
politics, I felt obliged to be in sympathy with the strikers. We
were organised by Mr and Mrs G. D. H. Cole. At Didcot I
stood about waiting to carry messages for the N.U.R., but
there were none to carry. At one of the private schools at which
I taught after having to leave Oxford without a degree, as so
many of us did in those days, the headmaster was an Old
Etonian and a Cambridge man; he was also, surprisingly, a
paid-up Communist Party member. Palme Dutt, Rust and
Campbell were my new leaders. I bought *Das Kapital* by
Marx in an English translation, but could never get beyond
the first two paragraphs. I subscribed to the *Worker's Weekly*
and liked to be seen reading it in public transport. The world
seemed to be drawing to a dawn where all men were equal, and
where in some way 'work of each for weal of all' would be done
for us by machinery, while we in happy equality pursued our
private hobbies. I was, in fact, a parlour pink, and bored by
politics. I was also Anglo-Catholic, and thought I had found
the solution of life in the teaching of Conrad Noel, the Red
Vicar of Thaxted, with his lovely incense-laden, banner-hung,
marigold-decorated church, with its folk-dancing and hand
weaving, going hand-in-hand with joyous religion, in what was
then unspoiled country. It was also a reawakening for me of an

interest in mediaeval churches. This time I visited them not just for their architecture, but also for their churchmanship. As I was earning my own living by now I was not often able to go abroad. My most rewarding experience thus was a visit to the Rhine and the Baroque Palaces of Germany and the Moravian settlement at Neuweid for its Easter ceremonies.

The more serious-minded told me the only important book on architecture was Geoffrey Scott's *Architecture of Humanism*. I did not find it easy reading. Of greater use was Christopher Hussey's *The Picturesque* (1927), which was the first book to burst away from Edwardian gardening to an appreciation of the parks and prospects created in the eighteenth century by Capability Brown. *Good and Bad Manners in Architecture* by A. Trystan Edwards (1924) was the first book to draw attention after the Great War to Regency architecture and to deplore the destruction of Nash's Regent Street. The countryside was being defended against spec. builders and advertisement hoardings and litter droppers by another pioneer in the appreciation of Georgian architecture, Clough Williams Ellis (*The Pleasures of Architecture* and *England and the Octopus*).

In those merry days of the late twenties and early thirties, it was still possible to find employment without passing examinations. Old friends pulled strings. My friend Maurice Bowra, then Dean of Wadham, approached the late Maurice Hastings, who first discovered the origin of the English Perpendicular style, and Maurice Hastings spoke to his quiet brother, Hubert de Cronin Hastings, and I was accepted on to the staff of *The Architectural Review*. It was all I could desire, though the salary was but £300 a year. I was sent round by Christian Barman, the nominal editor of the magazine, to architects' offices to fetch drawings and photographs to be reproduced. In this way I met Sir Edwin Lutyens, who was as welcoming as he was fascinating, and with the aid of a penny and a pencil drew the outlines of mouldings, and showed how a semicircle looked like half a tube, while a little less or a little more made all the difference. Arthur J. Davis of Mewes and Davis, was equally affable and instructive, and told me about how to make steps easy walking in hotels, and showed me his work at the Ritz. He was very dapper and businesslike and not at all the bow-tie tweedy type of architect with a pipe, which was the general run in those days. Frederick Etchells, who had recently been called in to help an architect out with the design of Crawford's building in Holborn, became a lifelong friend. I used to go and stay with him and his wife in Berkshire. His inspired monologues on architecture at last made me realise the difference between genuine modern and *moderne*. Etchells had translated Le Corbusier's *Vers Une Architecture*, which was compulsive and compulsory reading for all who were slightly Left and thought that nothing was quite so up to date as the architecture of France and Germany. Etchells had worked in the Omega workshops with Roger Fry, and as a Vorticist had contributed to a paper called *Blast*, with Wyndham Lewis and Pound. He had a great contempt for established architects and a great admiration for surveyors and civil engineers. He was also at heart in sympathy with the arts and crafts movement. Through the *Review* I became friends of these older arts and crafts architects, who were then regarded as anachronisms. I came to know old Mr Voysey in his little flat over Rumpelmeyer's off St James's Street; George Walton, then living in a flat in Westminster; Basil Oliver and two who remained friends to me to the end of their lives, J. N. Comper and M. H. Baillie Scott as already were John Summerson, Goodhart Rendel and Osbert Lancaster.

What made *The Architectural Review* a commercial success was its advertisement pages. These were for bronze doors, electroliers, paint, cement, stone and concrete. The editorial policy sometimes did not run in harness with the advertisers. In a mysterious way H. de C. Hastings, the real commander of *The Architectural Press* and its weekly, *The Architect's Journal*, caused the modern style to prevail. A profound influence on him and on us all was P. Morton Shand, an indefatigable, disillusioned and amusing journalist from Eton and Cambridge, and as famous as a judge of wine as he was of the modern architecture of Germany, Holland, Switzerland and Sweden. In the late twenties everything Swedish was admired. By the thirties the Dutch and the German took precedence, and the Bauhaus group was the most modern of all.

In the world of literature, I frequented the Squirearchy, as it was called, that is the group round that most generous and kindly of editors, J. C. Squire, who was the first person to publish a poem by me. His assistant was an Oxford friend, Alan Pryce Jones. Squire and Etchells, I thought so alike in appearance, that I asked them both to lunch, but when they were together they did not look quite the same, though their views on architecture coalesced.

It was through the entourage of J. C. Squire that I met Eric Gillett, and in conversation with him he thought of the book and its title. Arthur Waugh, head of Chapman & Hall, for whom Eric worked, had the courage to publish the book. I should add in case this appears too solemn an apologia, that architecture can be extremely funny, and that Osbert Lancaster, the Fleetwood-Hesketh brothers, Fredk Etchells, Michael Dugdale and John Summerson and my colleagues on *The Architectural Review*, added their wit to the enjoyment.

It was in this muddled state—wanting to be up to date but really preferring all centuries to my own—that I wrote this book, and in trying to defend myself, I seem almost to have written another.

July 1970                                              John Betjeman

# Chapter I · An Apostrophe to One of the Landed Gentry

*Pechasom gyd â'n tadau; gownaethom
gamwedd, anwireddus fuom.*—Psalmau

This I address to you as you are sitting in the library of your country house. The gun-room is dusty and the stables are deserted, you are fond of your library although you would not think of reading many of the books in it. The library is no longer a place of learning, it has become a place of refuge. It is enough for you to know that beyond the mouldering brick walls of the kitchen garden to the west, beyond the empty stables to the east, beyond the vast and unused kitchens to the south and beyond the curving drive surveyed by your library windows is about a mile of undulating park, buzzing with bees and cluster flies. But round the park the roaring tarmac roads coil. The steady humming and distant impatient hoots get nearer every year, as you sell and sell. Soon the cars and the people will be coming up the drive.

In your library there is no sign of the ancestors who founded your family. They lived in a house built for convenience before architecture became a self-conscious art. Their only memorials are in the church (removed by your grandfather from the old building at the 'restoration' of 1863); possibly these founders of your family brought prosperity to the village which still retains its mediaeval plan and unself-conscious cottages and barns.

In 1600 the old manor house disappeared and an ancestor built a fine building and called it The Hall. He ceased to care so much about the church, and thought more of travel and learning. His son bought books on travel, which saved him the trouble of going on long journeys. His fervent imagination was fired by poetical descriptions, mostly in verse, of Ind and Far Cathay. Possibly some of these books were removed from the old house when the library was built. If so, you have probably had to sell them. When your royalist seventeenth-century ancestor collected books, religious pamphlets were flying—by Penn and Muggleton, Whiston and Stillingfleet. There was more prose, and poetry was of a different sort. So in a few years your family had changed from one in Christendom to one in a nation. Once it had taken to buccaneering. Later it had preferred reading about buccaneers.

At the beginning of the eighteenth century the library in which you are standing was probably built. The heavy cornice with its fine plaster, the well-proportioned book-cases of carved oak and convenient shelves, the Italian marble mantelpiece and the long Venetian windows, were designed by some local architect who had studied Palladio and who had even met Inigo Jones. The plaster panel in the ceiling was left white until Sir James Thornhill should be passing that way, to lie on his back on a scaffold and paint a nice representation in it of your ancestor's wife, surrounded, in her semi-nudity, by cupids holding cream-like streamers. Meanwhile, more books were filling the library. Dogmatic, mystic or prophetic books on religion were being displaced by exquisitely printed folios of the classics. Curious and abusive pamphlets of Royalists and Puritans were put in the small shelves up near the ceiling, and in the lower shelves, level with the wainscoting were books on perspective and the drawings of Michael Angelo neatly engraved upon copper, and printed on fine thick Dutch paper which to this day preserves its consistency. The title-page was no longer cramped with ruled lines and a crowded summary of the contents of the book wedged in between them; the page contained few words and those large and exquisitely printed; after this would follow a second title page, this time engraved with some scene or patron's coat-of-arms. The books were becoming lavish, objects of beauty in themselves as well as repositories of information. Meanwhile the Puritan, with all this conscious art going on at the Hall, would murmur from his industrious farmhouse or forge 'Pagan . . . Pagan'.

By 1730 the son of the Hall is ready to go on his Grand Tour, and to come back with cloudy impressions of the new buildings of Italy and a detestation of the disorder of his own countryside. The village can remain where it is, with the cottages huddled round the church, although the church itself might do with a little improvement. That mutilated chancel screen can disappear; those old uncomfortable oak benches can be replaced with neat high boxes, in which one can sit at one's ease instead of being under the languorous eye of one's cousin the parson. One will even add a bit of art to the church and, when the old father dies, commission Roubiliac or Rysbrack up in

London to carve a fine tomb for him, representing Death with
a javelin aiming a blow at his old heart. Since the village is
untidy, this son of the Hall can at least set an example by
clearing up his own park. Those yew hedges which obscure the
garden front must be removed, and now that they are down,
how mean appears the front of the old house itself. The architect who had met Inigo Jones is in his grave, your ancestor's
father is in his dotage, so what harm can there be in adding a
new front? An architect from London who has published one
of those fine books that there are in the library comes down to
stay and suggests even further improvements. The new front is
finished, but it must look on something equally lovely. Remove
those trees, and clear away the home farm to some place further
from the wall, so that the ploughed field over there may not
interrupt the prospect. Now at the end of that long vista, which
will in forty years be neatly interspersed with beech clumps,
place a Roman temple. At the end of the lawn, where the grass
seems scarcely to change in quality with that below the ha-ha,
place some statue of Diana to catch the eye, and that will add
to the classic beauty of the place already created by the herd
of red deer. Near the red brick walled-in kitchen-garden,
whence that view of a bend in the river can be secured, let us
place a gazebo. And add on to this elevation of Clotworthy's
farm the two dimensional semblance of an arched colonnade.
Clotworthy will not mind. But the Puritan, who himself owns
a neighbouring farm to Clotworthy's, the Muggletonian black-
smith, the Calvinistic linen-draper in Tetbury, the Metho-
distical grocer in the same town and the enthusiastical parson

in the village church itself who has replaced the aged cousin will preach quite openly on 'The Paganism . . . the Wickedness . . . the Vanity of Riches at the Hall'.

In 1790 the son of the improver, the grandson of the builder of the seventeenth century house, is ready to go on the Grand Tour. He has already developed a taste for antiquarianism. In the library may be found books on numismatics alongside the editions of Mr Pope. And his father has regretted the money spent on improvements in his youth. He has become friendly with the enthusiastical parson, and the library is filled with books on the Calvinistic and Arminian controversy by Toplady, Wesley, Whitefield, and he has even had a visit from the Countess of Huntingdon, who has appraised his old age and heaped coals of fire upon his youth. But the son is never out of the library. There is one book which attracts him more than any. It is a two volume work on the antiquities of Athens by Messrs Stewart and Revett, architects; on his Grand Tour he will go beyond Rome to Greece, to the Parthenon, to Halicarnassus itself. He goes, and when he returns his father is dead and there is room for plenty of improvement in the Hall. A taste for the Gothic he has lately acquired through a slight acquaintance with William Beckford when on a visit to Spain, and Gothic is clearly the style for the English landscape. That temple can be replaced by a ruined Gothic arch which may be mistaken for the remains of a monastery. That wall of Clotworthy's farm, which looks so ridiculous with a colonnade, can be made to resemble a monument in the castellated style by the addition of some buttresses and crenellations. Clotworthy will not mind. But the congregation of Baptists, which was founded round the family at the farm, neighbouring on Clotworthy's, the large congregation of the Calvinistic Chapel in Tetbury, and the Methodist Chapel in the same town and the few atheists in the village itself; in fact, many people, except the parson and the churchmen, preach and pray against 'The wastefulness and the paganism . . . and the vanity at the Hall'. And they preach and pray to some purpose too about Paganism, because did not your ancestor at the Hall spend the last years of his life on an ingenious archaeological history of the county, in which he showed that the Druids who had set up the stones at Barbury Camp were the very same as the Ancient Greeks themselves? To this purpose he collected those unsaleable antiquarian books which fill more than half the shelves around you.

By 1830 the son of the Hall is not ready to go on the Grand Tour. What a disappointment this is to his old antiquarian father! The boy had been up in London. He had got into the set around the King. He preferred drinking, though his father did not grudge him that; he preferred gambling, though his father did not grudge him that; he preferred witty conversation, though his father did not grudge him that; but he had taken to politics and had no use for taste. Quite rightly he was opposed to the passing of the ridiculous Reform Bill. To add to the old man's trouble a merchant family had seen fit to come and live on the next estate. They had taken down the old farmhouse which had once been the manor of the next village. They had set up in its place an enormous yellow stucco mansion which, although he had to confess he admired the Greek detail and simplicity of the exterior, and the spacious and somewhat heavy furnishing within, was yet a little vulgar, a little too much 'all-of-a-piece', a little too devoid of learning to be entirely to his antiquarian taste. Moreover, his son took to these people, and even went so far as to marry the daughter. 'One knows people of that sort but one does not marry them.' The old man died.

His son, who had been an honest, open-hearted fellow, more given to politics than to education, was sorry about this. In 1840 he saw that the country was breaking up over the democrats. He joined the Oxford movement. That is why those quantities of tracts, somewhat ill-printed and badly bound, occupy the dusty shelves up at the top, alongside the earlier religious pamphlets. That is why the old church, too, was removed and that lavish structure, designed by Sir Gilbert Scott, put up in 1863 when the political son became old. Its prussian blue and light-red stained glass, its brass lectern, glistening encaustic tiles, reflected in the sticky pitch-pine benches, its hand-chiselled, yet conveniently mediaeval appearance was more suited to a ritualistic service than had been the inconvenient older building. Besides, the Vicar was a relation again. But the Atheists in the village, the Quakers at Clotworthy's neighbour's farm, the Ranters, who had supplanted the Calvinists in influence at Tetbury, and the Wesleyan New Connexion in the same town, the political club and the Benthamites all shouted against 'the ritualism, the class distinction, the idleness and the waste of money at the Hall.'

Although there might be what seemed a waste of money at the Hall, there was no waste of time. True to his generation this early Victorian father produced a large family of late Victorians. Some went to the bad and to the Colonies, some to the Church, and some married into their class, and acquired social position after their father's slight mistake; others made no effort to rectify it. One remained at home to look after the Hall. The library became dusty and was generally locked. A set of Lever, a set of Surtees, a set of Thackeray and one of Dickens were placed in a few empty shelves that remained, and thereafter the master's activities were confined to the gun-room. Here the chairs were of red leather, the walls were hung with antlers, as the walls of the main staircase hall with Landseers. The master was rarely off a horse and, when he was on his feet, he was rarely off conversation about horses.

To the hunt and to pedigree cattle your grandfather's interests turned. Food and drink were as plentiful as ever. Indoor animals and indoor vegetation far more so. But the end of the Hall was in sight. The Nonconformists in Tetbury, the Freethinkers in the village itself, and, what was far worse, the workmen in the far away towns and their representatives shouted 'The idleness, the class distinction at the Hall. . . . Tax it out of existence.' The idea of a Grand Tour was abandoned, unless a honeymoon in Italy and holidays in Switzerland or the South of France can be called Grand Tours.

So in 1932 you come to be standing in this library, the collection of all except your most recent ancestors. Your wife has found that the library is a well-proportioned room and plea-

santer to look at than the gun-room. It is useful, too, as some
of the old books are valuable and can be sold to dealers, and the
others can be sold by the ton or by the yard to America as wall
decoration, and so help to pay death duties. The old house is
too big to live in. Servants cannot be got, and the rooms are too
big to be 'cosy'. Except for the library, the house is shut up and
some of those kitchen quarters which are not in the basement
have been turned into living rooms. As a last wall between you
and the civilisation (if such it can be called) that is soon going
to get the better of you is the park and the high-walled kitchen
garden. Outside the gates and close to the lodge is a petrol
station. 'Hideous,' you say, yet what would you do for getting
about if it were not there? Part of the park has been sold for
building strips of villas. 'Ghastly,' you say, yet what would you
do without the money that came from them? All round the
estate are roaring main roads. 'The noise!' you exclaim. Yet
what would you do if they were winding and untarred? The
country is not what it was to you. You pay enormous taxes to
a State which is bent on destroying your position. The convenience of your house is solely that of shelter. The telephone
(carried by prominent poles that stride down the eighteenth-
century vista) is ringing all day. You are rarely in. You are
always seeing friends. Your house is too large and unmovable.
You almost want to get rid of it.

Here are the two sorts of life. Historically separated from
one another by the nineteenth century, the transition period.
What can you do to reconcile them? Preservation of the
countryside is but an ineffective compromise. Clotworthy is

dead, and his sons make motorbikes in the Midlands. The
praying of the Nonconformists has been heard and even their
own establishments are threatened. The democrats and the
freethinkers are in. They no longer shout and preach, they are
coming up the drive in their motor cars. You are already half a
democrat yourself.

# Chapter II · The Argument of the Book

*Ambition sigh'd: she found it vain to trust*
*The faithless Column and the crumbling Bust:*

*Convinc'd, she now contracts her vast design*
*And all his triumphs shrink into a Coin.*

Pope, *Moral Essays, Epistle V*

The first chapter of this book was in the nature of an apostrophe. Those who have understood it need go no further, for the succeeding chapters are but elaborations of the opening theme; those who did not understand it need go no further, since the elaborations will not help them. There is little reason for my continuing the rest of the book beyond pleasing my publisher, and indulging my own pleasure in writing and gaining that money which I cannot come by honestly. Architecture suffers by never being dealt with in pamphlets—always in books. A page of illustrations of good and bad buildings will do more than a chapter of text. Here is another textbook, an opportunity for the thousands of 'art critics', of whom I am unwillingly one, to air their pedantry and express their annoyance, an opportunity for aesthetic snobs to contest yet another theory; but if one copy of this book goes to every Institute for the Training of Museum Officials, for Preserving the Countryside, for Affiliating Incorporated Painter-Stainers, for Painting and Staining Incorporated Institutes, and to every other body for the official expression of aesthetic self-consciousness, I shall have made enough money to get myself up in an arty manner, and so qualify for a lectureship at some Ruskin School of Art, there to pronounce dicta admired and uncriticised for the rest of my life—an acknowledged 'expert' whose opinion will be valuable to Americans. I believe it is Adrian Stokes who says that when art criticism is rampant, art is moribund. And certainly no one would be fool enough to think that a painter or an architect was ever inspired to creative work by art criticism. The disastrous results of the more typical art and architectural school products should be proof enough of that.

No, this book is written for two reasons. Primarily to dissuade the average man from the belief that he knows nothing about architecture, and secondly to dissuade the average architect from continuing in his profession. In order to accomplish the first task, I opened with an apostrophe which anyone can read without feeling abashed at his abysmal ignorance. To accomplish the second task I brought the word 'taste' into the title of my book as a sure draw for the average architect who always considers himself a practical man of it. But both tasks will have failed, for the work is not a novel which will please the average man, and not enough wrapped up in technical terms for the average architect. Today with regard to architecture the average man is a fool and the average architect is a snob.

'Of course, I'm not in a position to criticise,' says the man in the street, as he gazes up at a colossal hideosity aping the style of Queen Anne, or neatly portraying in yellow and red terra cotta an enlarged edition of a seventeenth-century merchant's house in Delft. 'Of course, I'm not in a position to criticise—but it's always seemed to me a fine building—not altogether practical of course, for us who have to work in it, the rooms are a bit dark—but it's imposing—that's what it is—imposing.'

'Mind you, you're an architect—and I don't know—but it seems to me there's some fine things going up nowadays—this is only five years old, you know—the papers said it was magnificent.' Nevertheless, in the eighteenth century, when the average man did not exist, every gentleman of property felt himself in a position to criticise, and every person without it felt himself in a position to admire. In those days people minded about architecture and took a pride in it. They welcomed an opportunity to build, for a building would improve the landscape; now, how common is the expression, 'What a pity—they're going to build there.' Nor is the average man, whose tasteful little residence shouts its ostentation across the tram-lines to the other side of the main road, entirely to blame for his lack of interest in architecture. Although he lives in a hideous suburb, surrounded by it, walking through it to his office, although he works in an ill-ventilated closet of polished mahogany and bevelled glass where the decoration is continually sticking into him, worrying his eyesight, still he does not notice architecture. Nature is kind. She causes her creatures to adapt themselves to their surroundings; to certain fish in the deepest parts of the ocean she gives enormous eyes which are able to pierce the darkness of the watery deep. To the town-

dweller to-day she has given a kind of eye which makes him
blind to the blatant ugliness by which he is surrounded. She
has affected his critical reasoning powers and his eyesight.
Nature is kind, and it is not for me in this book to attempt
to reverse her laws. Rather I must explain why they have been
reversed.

The average man is but in part to blame, the architect more
so. Unfortunately most architects are average men themselves.
In my own unpleasant occupation of architectural journalism
I am continually meeting architects. Although they are average
men, average architects are average individualists. Although
intensely proud of being in a 'profession'—the word 'trade'
gives architects an upper middle-class shudder—they are intensely jealous of one another. Their camaraderie is limited to
the golf club. If you meet the average architect you will not be
able to tell him from the average man. He will pull in at his
pipe and puff out the opinions of *The Times* and the *Daily
Express*. As a 'professional' man he will keep a brave face in
front of the oncoming starvation which is threatening most
architects; like any other 'professional' man, his talk will be
tinged with that class consciousness which is so frequently
mistaken for Conservatism. The average architect is good to
his children, loyal to his wife, sometimes he is a good practical
builder, often he is a good practical draughtsman, always he is
a 'professional' man. The 'professional man' comes before the
artist, and, of course, long before the builder and the mason.
Because he is an average man, the average architect is blind
and subject to those laws of nature which I have already men-

tioned. If he were not subject to them, the City of London would not look like what it does at present, the main streets of our provincial towns would not exist in their present form, nor would Kingsway, Regent Street, the Thames Embankment; the suburbs would have been planned before they were built, Crewe would have been a paradise and Leeds a garden city. Snobbery would not have existed between builder and engineer and architect. They would all have been one man. As it is, they are all different men, each with a vague idea of the other's trade, and each attempting to be a jack-of-all trades. East Ham, Swindon, Huddersfield, Manchester, Colindale, New Cross, Ilford, Liverpool Street and Marylebone Station are the result. Not far from the ill-ventilated room where I do my uninteresting work is an architect's office. There I see a gentleman in pince-nez take off his cuffs and sit down by a drawing-board; presently a 'cheerioh-old-boy-one-over-the-eight-last-night-high-jinks-in-Finchley' young man comes in and puts an over all over his plus-fours. He too sits at a drawing-board, somewhat listlessly. Their employer—and the employer of many more such draughtsmen—comes in at about eleven after a busy previous night 'getting clients' or fishing for a knighthood, or advertising himself on committees. It is in the hands of these inspired gentlemen, whose fervour runs away with them, whose discontent with the present situation causes them to be almost mad with idealism, whose anxiety to build Jerusalem has expressed itself in their white-hot excitement, it is in the hands of these gentlemen, dear readers, that the noble service of architecture lies. That uninspired underling with

the pince-nez and the celluloid cuffs, that top-hole lad who
once went to the Forty-Three when he was a student at the
Architectural Association, that gentlemanly person who gets
himself up as a tactful compromise between a major-general
and a business man—those three know, of course, all about
economics, engineering, town-planning, the history of art, and
sanitation; they are sufficiently imaginative to weld their
knowledge into a coherent whole; they are sufficiently devoid
of petty jealousy to be able to co-operate with others with the
same ideas. They are madly keen to get to work to save the
world. They have the tact of a Wren, the taste of a Chambers,
the originality of a Soane.

> *Oh judgment, thou art fled to brutish beasts*
> *And men have lost their reason—*

It is not because I have such a rooted dislike for English
architects, but because I have such a rooted love for English
architecture that I write so malevolently of the majority of its
present practisers in this country. The importance of architure is immeasurable; its history, whether looked at in detail
by counties, in part by countries or in whole by the world, is
extraordinary. Book after book has appeared, to attempt to
define it, yet no definition has been reached. Perhaps the best
attempt to define it was made by Sir Thomas Jackson, whose
book *Architecture* is so much better than were his buildings:

> Architecture is based on building, as poetry may in a
> manner be said to be based on prose. But architecture is

something more than building, and poetry something more than prose. What is it in each case that is added to make the difference? . . . What has the barbarian done to make this transition from mere building to architecture? What has he added? Certainly not ornament. He has added an idea. He has brought reason to bear upon practice, and this influence once begun and carried on with advancing skill, is the secret of all that followed.

The beginning of architecture in its humblest form may serve to illustrate a great truth that should never be lost sight of in tracing the history of the art in its progress from style to style. It is this, that all great changes through which architecture passed successively may, as a rule, be found to have originated in suggestions of utility and convenience. Thus Architecture was developed from structural necessities and suggestions, not by addition of ornament to structural form, as some would have it, but by binding structural forms themselves into forms of beauty. . . . Nowhere did Architecture declare its independence of ornament more vigorously than in the Cistercian buildings of the twelfth and thirteenth centuries. By the rules of that stern order, ornament was absolutely forbidden. There were to be neither painting nor sculpture; the glass was to be white, without cross or ornament, and the bell tower was to be low and unostentatious. Like the Mussulman, the Cistercian artist was deprived of the use of natural ornament. At the most, he could temper the dry severity of the arches of door and window by moulding the edges, and abroad, where

moulding was less in fashion then with us, as for instance in
Burgundy, in such churches as that at Pontigony, there was
but little of that. But notwithstanding this prohibition, the
Cistercian has shown us that he could dispense with ornament, and wanted nothing but nicety of proportion, dignity
of scale, graceful outline in the forms of his construction to
enable him to reach the highest level in his art. The Yorkshire abbeys are mostly Cistercian, and are among the
loveliest buildings and the stateliest that have come down
to us from the Middle Ages.

To return to our definitions. What is Architecture? Architecture does not consist in beautifying building, but on the
contrary in building beautifully, which is quite another
thing. . . . As prose rises into poetry by the greater elevation of thought, the finer flow of language, the touch of
sympathy, grace and pathos, so does building pass into
Architecture with the superior grace of the main forms of the
fabric, perfect expression of the conditions of the construction
and closer harmony between purpose and achievement.

In a word—Architecture is the poetry of construction.

After reading such illuminating and excellent writing as this,
it seems odd that Sir Thomas Jackson should have been a
lover of the Jacobean and have built the regrettable Examina-
tion Schools which are such an odd addition to the famous
High Street of Oxford.

For all that excellent definition which I have just quoted, I
do not believe architecture can be defined. An attempt at

definition can help us to understand it. So many factors are concerned with it, the planning of towns, the increase of population, the conditions of life, the climate, the subsoil, the political tendencies of the people, their aesthetic desires—the whole question of whether a community is influenced by its architecture or architecture by the community—that it is useless to attempt to define it. Sir Thomas Jackson has explained the reasons for getting pleasure out of a seemly building, but he has not explained why the building is there, nor how closely the dress of its inhabitants, their vehicles, and their instruments are connected with its architecture. Nor can he be expected to do so. Architecture cannot be understood by a definition. Some of its beauty may be grasped by an history of it.

For this reason I am attempting to trace its development in England. I cannot hope to define it. I only hope to cause some interest in it.

Briefly my argument is this. Before the Reformation, or even earlier, when all Europe was united in an age of faith, the Church was the dominant force in architecture. For this reason architectural style changed with the opinions of the Church; and all Europe was Christendom, with Holy Church for its expression of consciousness. With the Renaissance and a vague archaeological hankering after classical learning, individuality and doubt, which made themselves felt in the last days of the age of faith, found a means of expression. The intellectual and spiritual muddle is expressed in England by the Jacobean style. As learning came to be more admired and less

feared, and reason came into its own, we got the architecture
of the age of reason—the work of Wren, of Gibbs, of Kent, of
Chambers. There are, of course, exceptions to these seemingly
dangerous generalisations. With the dawn of learning developed
the system of class consciousness; knighthood and the blind
feudalism of the age of faith had vanished. Englishmen desired
the then awe-inspiring experience of travel, and Jacobean
architecture is often rather like a traveller's hazy impressions.
Then with that acute social battle of the Cavaliers and Roundheads, class consciousness in England established itself with
the monarchy. Architecture fell into the hands of the upper
classes, and there for over 100 years it remained. The work of
Wren, Gibbs, Kent and Chambers is the work of an Upper
Class. And by 'Upper Class' I mean the educated, not neces-
sarily the well-born. With the Regency the Upper Classes
made some concessions to the growing industralists, and we
have architects who do not confine themselves to building
mansions, churches and hospitals, but who are interested in
town planning, and who build streets, terraces, squares,
circuses and shops.

After the Reform Bill the Middle Class, which represents
industrialism, took control—or rather lost control—of the fine
Regency tradition. The rest of the book must be a sad but
exciting history of the chaos that resulted. The only hope that
I can put forward is that England will emerge from its present
state of intense individualism and become another Christendom. Not until it is united in belief will its architecture regain
coherence. That union cannot come until a return of Chris-

tendom. Whether that Christendom will be a Union of Soviet Republics, a League of Socialistic Nations or an Ecclesiastical Union, it is not for me to say. I only know, like everyone else, that we are changing in a rapid and terrifying manner to some new form of civilisation which will demand new architectural expression. Perhaps we are rushing towards annihilation. In that case there will be no architecture at all. For me that is the most satisfactory solution.

# Chapter III · Christendom

O tell of His might,
  O sing of His grace,
Whose robe is the light,
  Whose canopy space;
His chariots of wrath
  The deep thunder clouds form,
And dark is His path
  On the wings of the storm.

Sir Robert Grant, *Hymns A. and M.*

I am pleasantly awoken every morning in London by the sound of a church bell at eight o'clock. It sounds above the early lorries and rides triumphant over the roaring engines being warmed up in the garage of the street behind me, before the chauffeurs depart to fetch their precious masters to the office. And every morning as this bell rings, one elderly sexton, two old ladies and a pale youth attend the daily communion—or mass, as it is called among Anglo-Catholics—in St Agatha's. During the day the church remains open, and some more old women and some

*Young men, that no one knows, go in and out*
*With a far look in their eternal eyes.*

But out of every 500 people who go down my street, I do not think it would be inaccurate to say that less than three call in at St Agatha's.* When the bell rings and wakes me in the morning, even though I am tired, I envy the young man and the two old women and the sexton their faith, that will let them face the discomfort of early rising for a mystic experience in St Agatha's to carry them through the day. That early morning bell is symbolic of the lost age of faith; the symbolism becomes even more pathetic when, twenty minutes after the eight o'clock bell, six strokes on the sanctus tell the people cleaning the gramophone shop and the men at the 'Lex Garage' opposite that the Son of Man died to save the world, and has died again just across the road today.

Church art today is at a low ebb, and it is hard to believe that the faith which built St Agatha's (which is, by the way, an impressive building of Edwardian date) created the Romanesque and Gothic architecture, which remain more lasting memorials to Catholicism than the frail old women who represent English Catholicism today. The church was an ideal to work for; its fierce energy and its increasing multiplicity of outward symbols in the mediaeval age created the energy of the Norman style and the multiplicity of the Gothic.

In those happy days, when man did not have a mind of his own, the king ruled the baron, the baron the yeoman, the yeoman the serf, and the Church ruled all. Happy days of feudalism when the greatest injustice was not that the serf was starved and the baron overtaxed, but that the Ottomans occupied Jerusalem! Happy days of feudalism, before nation rose against nation, when death and torture and oppression were

* St Anselm's, Davis Street, by Balfour and Turner.

compensated for in heaven and when the wicked were cast into hell! Happy days of feudalism, when a local saint daily somewhere in Christendom performed a miracle, and when Christ might come in person round the next corner! With such an all-powerful representative on earth as Holy Church, with such a living rock upon which she was built, is it surprising that no spire could be too high, no decoration too costly, no nave too broad, no altar too filled with precious stones, for the worship of a God who gave his rewards, if not in this life, at least in the next? With the certainty of heaven, did it matter to the architect and the mason, that their names were forgotten? Their reward was in their work, and their eternal rest with the saints whose images they carved on the west fronts of Lincoln, Wells and Salisbury, and in the porches and towers and side-chapels of their village churches. Although we know that William of Sens was the designer of the major part of the choir in Canterbury Cathedral, we do not know who was the carver of the capitals therein. The Gothic architects sunk their individuality in their faith.

And because in the Middle Ages architects were not generally cursed with a desire to perpetuate their names to posterity, and because they lacked the mammon of unrighteousness 'individuality' which we so much admire, Holy Church took over their works and crystallised their aspirations. And as faith can move mountains, so nothing was impossible to Holy Church and the energetic masons, carvers, designers and jewellers of which she was comprised. The round arches and flat roofs of the Normans were not enough for the Plantagenets, just as the grace of Saxon architecture and draughtsmanship had not been enough for William the Conqueror. The delicate creative genius of the oppressed Saxons struggled through and expressed itself in Gothic architecture. Without any self-conscious change Gothic architecture grew out of the Norman or Romanesque. The faith of Holy Church could not be encased in mere stone. The stone must soar with her. And the height of her soaring was the pointed arch.

For this reason the genius of Gothic architecture comes out in the fascinating history of the pointed arch. There are several theories as to its origin and that of the ribbed vaulting characteristic of Gothic architecture. In the romantic days, when our rude native architecture was thought to have been rediscovered by its Beckfordian exponents, it was argued that the shady lengths of the cathedral naves were an attempt to portray in stone, avenues in forests whose trees met in a point overhead. The theory of the Romanticist gave way to that of the pedant, and for a long time it was imagined that the intertwining of the rounded Norman arches suggested the pointed arch to Gothic architects. It has, moreover, always been contended that the pointed arch came from the East. And certainly the pointed arch was no new discovery, for it was used in the seventh century in the Dome of the Rock and the Mosque of El-Aksa at Jerusalem. In Egypt it is to be seen in Coptic churches of the sixth century. It is therefore generally supposed that pointed or Gothic architecture received its impetus from the Crusaders, starting in Sicily and spreading through Italy to France, and thence at last to England, where the early pointed style appears at Fountains Abbey, which was built in the twelfth century.

Although Western architects may have realised, from hearing about or from seeing Eastern examples, that the pointed arch was a possibility, all who understand these principles of Gothic architecture, which Ruskin and Le Corbusier have expounded, will not be able to credit a theory which makes the Gothic architects mere imitators. For the most part they were engineers in stone, as all their buildings demonstrate, from the immense Salisbury Cathedral spire (1331) to that Crystal Palace of stone and glass, King's College Chapel, Cambridge (1450). And when we consider that Fountains Abbey, one of the first English buildings to possess a pointed arch, was of Cistercian foundation, and that the stern Cistercians set no store by decoration, depending always on beauty of proportion and the glory of ingenious construction for their effect, I think it seems more unlikely still that the pointed arch was a mere innovation from the East.

The manner in which the Gothic architect evolved the pointed arch and the ribbed vaulting characteristic of his style is best described by that admirable and already quoted writer, Sir Thomas Jackson.

The main difficulty arose from the round arch, which being an inelastic form could not be adapted to irregular heights, and the solution was found in the adoption of the pointed arch, which admitted of being raised to various heights as the circumstances required. This overcame the difficulty of the arches which could now be brought to suitable levels and be made equal at the crown. But it left the difficulty of the carved surfaces of the vaulting worse than ever. These surfaces were too irregular to meet symmetrically on regular lines, for they needed to be twisted and tilted to come together at all, and so it was that the system of strengthening the lines of intersection by ribs was invented. The surfaces could not be brought together except by such twisting and winding as to be dangerous, and therefore ribs were constructed on the lines of true arches, and the panels of the vaulting were fitted between them, and rest on them securely, even when these surfaces wind. Vaulting thus became a system of ribs and panels; the ribs forming a framework or skeleton, which is clothed by a covering or ceiling of light masonry, which however, from its arched form, has a constructive strength of its own.

All the thrust outward and downward of such heavy vaulting as this was, therefore, concentrated on the columns which supported it. As it was impossible to build any large enough to bear such a weight—for the thick round Norman columns had, like all Norman buildings, notoriously insecure foundations— the Gothic architects solved the problem in quite another way. They made the supporting columns comparatively slender, and the outward thrust of the vaulting they counter-balanced by a flying buttress pressing into the column from the exterior of the building. A well-known example of this form of construction may be seen in Westminster Abbey.

As their skill in this delicate art of thrust and counter-thrust grew, the necessity for an obvious flying buttress was removed by the systems of *lierne* and *fan* vaulting. This last development of Gothic vaulting Jackson describes as follows:

> An example of the *lierne* vault at Winchester will show how the whole surface of the vault came to consist of a network of ribs, great and small in every interval of which a separate 'filling-in' piece had to be fitted. It may easily be understood that the least settlement of a pier would disarrange this elaborate puzzle-work and make some of the pieces loose. . . . It was this, no doubt, that suggested uniting rib and panel in one substance, a plan that of course upset the whole theory of rib and panel vaulting. The entire vault now became a shell of solid masonry; the ribs, instead of carrying the vault, became mere surface ornaments, mere panelling, decorating the underside of the vault, and no longer elements of the construction.

This is called *fan* vaulting, which started with Gloucester Cathedral cloisters (1351–1412), one of the most beautiful features of that most beautiful and interesting of all English mediaeval cathedrals. It later appeared in King's College Chapel (1447) and St George's Chapel, Windsor (1508), and Henry VII's Chapel at Westminster (1512). The latest example is at Christ Church, Oxford, where the whole vaulting over an enormous staircase leading to the dining-hall seems to rest on a single column and the surrounding walls. This architectural freak was the work of Dr Fell and a London architect named Smith, and was completed in 1630, long after classical architecture had begun to reign.

I have gone into detail in describing the process of Gothic vaulting to show that the architects of our mediaeval cathedrals, who are generally considered rude and ignorant old retainers of a superstitious religion, were in reality highly skilled engineers. There is no difference between the genius which erected the Crystal Palace or the newest battleship and the genius which built King's College Chapel or St George's Chapel, Windsor. The one used steel, the other stone. The sentimentalising of Gothic architecture into a form of elementary archaeology suitable for the middle forms in schools, combined with the unfortunate efforts which we see everywhere, of the so-called Gothic revivalists, has made the word 'Gothic' anathema to the average modern appreciator of architecture. I remember at school receiving lectures on Norman fonts. Such lectures were to most people very naturally boring, and have contributed considerably to the general decline in the study of architecture in this country. If some well-meaning canon delivers a talk on the English cathedrals in a school, he will inevitably go into detail about ye Quainte olde Pryore Lanfranc, who boughte ye silver crosse for ye high altar for two shillings, as though such a picturesque fact had anything to do with architecture. In the same spirit he will show illustrations of gargoyles and of the more elaborate intricacies, frequently hideous, of Gothic decorative detail, with such remarks as that we cannot carve like that nowadays. It is such talk as this that leads people to believe that nothing is good unless it is hand done. It leads people to believe that Gothic architecture is a quaint survival that cannot be done nowadays, to which the obvious answer is

that it *cannot* be done nowadays, and anyone would be a fool
and wastrel who would attempt to build a Gothic building in
stone or brick today.

It is this admiration for a Gothic arch or a Norman window
which leads people on local councils to sacrifice convenience
and any Georgian building to some trumpery piece of Early
English tracery, built into a wall in the main street of a town.
The same spirit caused the Bishop of London to pull down a
lovely little eighteenth-century church in the City, called St
Catherine Coleman, within the last few years, on the ground
that it was modern (1741) and undistinguished. St Catherine
Coleman contained the old box pews, the galleries, the clear
glass and the fittings—those relics of a sturdy, departing Protestantism, which are hardly to be found anywhere else in the
country, and which are an ornament to the eighteenth century,
that great period in our history. Nevertheless, the neighbouring
church of St Helen's, Bishopsgate, was not even condemned
with the other nineteen 'modern' and Wren City churches
which were to be taken down in 1921. This building survived
the fire and is therefore 'old'. It does not matter that it was
ravaged by the Victorians, that it is no more distinguished than
the average country church, of which there are thousands of
examples everywhere. It is of 'historical and antiquarian interest', and therefore must be preserved. I will have more to
say of the present state of ecclesiastical art in a later chapter; at
present it is enough to say that the Gothic architects who built
St Helen's would have viewed with dismay the last century's
spoliation of their work, and would certainly have preferred

that St Catherine Coleman should be preserved, Protestant though it was, than the farce of preserving another building just because it was 'old'.

Mediaeval architects were innovators and experimentalists, despite or rather because of their faith. Gothic has fallen into the hands of antiquarianism, and architecture and the dead had of that grisly science are generally considered by the public to be identical. Those well-meaning canons who lecture, those preservation-mad town councillors who obstruct, and those dreary Wykehamical antiquarians have preponderated in their opinions for long enough. No Gothic architect could have borne with them.

Maybe Gothic architecture has been so misrepresented because of the extreme remoteness of the ages in which it was built. The Middle Ages are even harder for us to understand than the nineteenth century. And that is putting the matter as strongly as possible. The eighteenth and seventeenth centuries are much nearer. We cannot live in the silence which surrounded past ages in English history. No part of England is today so remote that one can sit in it for half an hour without hearing somewhere the hoot of a train or the roar of car and motor bicycle. Today in Ireland it is certainly possible sometimes to find silence among those remote inland counties, where the colour-washed towns will be full of jennet-, donkey- and horse-drawn carts of a market day, and when on every other day of the week houses and fields are still as the bare hills. And today in Ireland something of the faith of the Middle Ages prevails. To people who live in small cabins among wastes of bog and water, closed in by hills and only approached by uneven lonely roads, the silence brings a faith. The hills have personalities, the hawthorn hedges are full of fairies, the rowan trees keep evil from the threshold, and the voices of heavy swans that fly across the distance are the singing of departed spirits. Today we call such beliefs superstition. But if we in England consisted, as we did once, of scattered communities huddled between a silent earth and sky, disturbed only by the noises of animals and the elements, we would readily believe in ghosts and evil, and though our vehicles moved slower, our minds might progress a little faster in unearthly things. And as the horse carried us through empty forests or over stormy downs, we might realise that man can be driven as much by the fear which follows him behind as by the more pleasant hopes, affections and aspirations that lead him on. It is not for me or for anyone to say that the old way of living is 'better' than the present, or that a community which lived in stone dwellings, clustered firmly round an ancient church, is more permanent than the community which lives in motor cars and small flats and houses taken on a short lease. I am only emphasising the remoteness of mediaevalism and the futility of attempting to preserve its methods, planning or buildings in an urban civilisation.

In the village of Thaxted, in Essex, there has been an attempt, not unsuccessful, to centre the life of the place round the catholic service of the church. The church has become a place of importance once more, not a seedy relic continually needing repairs to the chancel; there is some reason for the

numerous footpaths which lead to it, dotted across the ord-
nance map; and the footpaths are not always straight. Church
social life was not originally confined to tea-parties and Dorcas
Societies. At Thaxted, the public-house is not looked upon as a
place of sin. Yet, despite the religious atmosphere of Thaxted
Church, and despite the communal life centring round it and
the able and great character of Conrad Noel, the incumbent,
one realises that it is only in remote agricultural districts that
faith, as the mediaeval church knew it, stands any chance of
surviving. Therefore one cannot blame the canons who lecture
and the preservation-mad town councillors and the Wyke-
hamists for treating Gothic architecture in terms of mediaeval
archaeology. Every village with its cottages clustered round its
church is a relic. For the cottagers have moved to the towns,
and the cottages are filled with arty escapists who are trying to
blind themselves with the past, and the workers are in the
cinema in Stortford, or on their motor bicycles, or listening to
the wireless, or reading Lord Castlerosse or James Douglas
in the *Sunday Express*, when the bell for service rings. But do
not blame the vicar, he is no longer a man with authority.
Blame the age, for that is the only thing which can frighten
you. The age has lost one faith, but it does not yet seem to have
found another.

34

# Chapter IV · The Upper Classes Take Over from Holy Church

*Set me fine Spanish tables in the hall;*
*See they be fitted all;*
*Let there be room to eat*
*And order taken that there want no meat.*
*See every sconce and candlestick made bright,*
*That without tapers they may give a light.*

*Look to the presence: are the carpets spread,*
*The dazie o'er the head,*
*The cushions in the chairs,*
*And all the candles lighted on the stairs?*
*Perfume the chambers, and in any case*
*Let each man give attendance in his place!*

Anonymous, *Christ Church MS*.

Not only the Lollards, but also the wanderers across the sea, were the cause of the break-up of the age of faith. Knowledge, as God said, was the fruit of evil. The Renaissance was as great an enemy to the Romanist faith as Communism is to capitalism. The 'humanities', the knowledge of classical Latin and Greek, were associated with the desire of man to free himself from superstition. The inevitable self-consciousness which waylays a man, as soon as he has been freed from some bonds whether ethical or economic, waylaid the blushing English adventurer who was unable fully to understand the discoveries of the Renaissance. Not every Englishman can be a Bacon, a Wyclif or a Shakespeare. And, although some brilliant exceptions showed themselves in the world of letters in England, it was not until Inigo Jones' and Wren's time that architecture was able to express itself in the scholarly manner of the Renaissance. Until then what is known as Jacobean and Elizabethan architecture remained the architecture of doubt.

The dissolution of the monasteries was not the death blow to Gothic architects. The class ascendancy, which took the place of church ascendancy, needed an architecture too. Barons were no longer in need of fortified castles, for a culture from the sunny courts of Italy filled all intelligent men in England with a desire for sunny courts and culture in their own country. Those that had the money built themselves palaces, which to this day are the last beautiful effort of architects unaffected by the humanistic or Renaissance tradition. Their plain brick buildings set about with lawns and clipped yew and box, surveyed by oriel windows and arranged in an orderly plan within and without, have caused the 'Tudor' style to be the cause since of many a hopeless revival.

The older colleges at Oxford are examples of the Tudor style, with the low courtyard of students' rooms broken by chapel and the dining-hall rising out of the low blocks surrounding them. Not unlike the colleges were the manor houses of the sixteenth century, the domestic expression of Perpendicular architects who have become secular even in their church building. The courtyard round which the manor was built was entered by a gate tower, and on the opposite side stood the great hall and buttery and kitchen; to the right of this a with-drawing room and a chapel, on the left of the courtyard, bed-rooms. Tudor manors were built after a monastic plan, and in the beginning, life in them was a sort of secular monasticism, servants and masters eating in the same room, and all collected and working within the narrow limits of the manor itself.

As travel grew popular and class consciousness grew greater, the ordered group-life of the manor split up into sections. Labourers returned to the village, the chapel and chaplain were removed and religious life centred in the parish church until, by the eighteenth century, vast houses were planned, with ground floors and first floors full of fine rooms for the gentry, and dark basements and squalid attic bedrooms for the servants. The gentry had come under the influence of learn-ing, they would no longer be amused by or interested in their dependents, as they were in the days of Shakespeare and before him. The servants were still too much of a group, blinded by a faith in the gentry, to notice the discomfort in which they lived. Industrialism, the knowledge of the machine, a harder and more cruel learning than that of Latin and Greek, was first to rouse them from their torpor. And those who were roused built themselves hideous miniatures of the life they once had witnessed, with parlour, bedrooms and labour-saving kit-chenette. They became the middle classes, and Leeds and Sheffield and the suburbs of London are full of them. A whole book could be written on the social conscience as shown in the plan of the house. I expect some German or some Don has written it.

Nevertheless, I doubt whether there can be found a complete Tudor domestic building today which was unaffected by the learning of the Renaissance. The pedantry of Lyly in his *Euphues*, the scholasticism which Shakespeare parodied, the concrete equivalent of Holophernes' 'honorificabilitudinitatibus' appeared in decoration. Though the architects remained steady enough, as, until the last century in England, they always have done, the old craftsmen who carved the reredos and capitals on cathedrals went off their heads. Nor is it surprising. Their new master, his lordship, brought back a book of Italian designs boldly engraved on wood, spaciously printed and bound in tooled leather and neatly kept flat by a gorgeous metal clasp. 'Copy these,' said he, 'I will have them about the doors, and on the panelling and on the ceiling.' And copy them they did. The results are the curious designs now known vaguely as Jacobean or Elizabethan, exquisite in workmanship and colour, often vile in proportion.

So important a part did decoration play in the post-Reformation house that quite soon, with the employment of foreign designs and frequently foreign craftsmen, architecture and decoration were for the first time in England divorced. The mason who built the fine brick chimney stack, and the glazier who constructed the grand windows of his lordship's new mansion, knew little of what was going on inside. Decoration became for a time what it has become today, an applied form of ornamentation, a separate trade to cover up the 'ugly bare patches' left by architecture. For this reason Jacobean is cheap and easy to copy today. The ornament can now be machine-made and bought by the yard, and glued on to a simple wooden framework at the minimum of expense.

When faith was abandoned at the beginning of the Renaissance period in England, men did not know where to look for shackles. They could find for a time no medium for self-expression. Early Renaissance architecture in England represents their state of chaos. When a faith has been for centuries a living faith, its upheaval results not only in a common discontent and restlessness, but also in a muddled, restless architecture. I see in the years of religious doubt immediately following the Reformation, before men's minds became accustomed to the monarchical government that was finally to be established under William and Mary for 200 years, a parallel with our own time. Today industrialisation and aristocratic government have become incompatible; the way out offered by Communism seems to be going too far; we are without shackles again and cannot find any in a compromise. The difference is again a religious one, although it may be expressed in different terms. Our own conflict between jazz-modern and monumental Queen Anne, the one as stupid and uncomprehending as the other, is similar to the struggle between the architecture of faith and the architecture of humanism which went on from 1550 to 1650.

Luther had stimulated thought all right, but he had not gone far enough, and the logical conclusion seemed a little like hell; just as Communism seems a little like hell to the individualist today, so individualism seemed like hell to the Catholic group-conscious mind after the Reformation. This state of mind is expressed by Tawney in *Religion and the Rise of Capitalism*:

The difference between loving men as a result of first loving God, and learning to love God through a growing love
of men, may not at first sight appear profound. To Luther it
seemed an abyss, and Luther was right. It was, in a sense,
nothing less than the Reformation itself. For carried, as it
was not carried by Luther, to its logical result, the argument
made, not only good works, but sacraments and the church
itself unnecessary. . . . Its effects on social theory were
staggering. Since salvation is bestowed by the operation of
grace in the heart and by that alone, the whole fabric of
organised religion, which had mediated between the individual soul and its Maker—divinely commissioned hierarchy,
systematised activities, corporate institutions—drops away
as the blasphemous trivialities of a religion of works. The
mediaeval conception of the social order, which had regarded it as a highly articulated organism contributing in
their different degrees to a spiritual purpose, was shattered,
and differences which had been distinctions within a larger
unity were set in irreconcilable antagonism to each other.
Grace no longer completed nature: it was the antithesis of it.
Man's actions as a member of society were no longer the
extension of his life as a child of God: they were its negation.
Secular interests ceased to possess even remotely, a religious
significance: they might compete with religion, but they
could not enrich it. Detailed rules of conduct—a Christian
casuistry—are needless or objectionable: the Christian has a
sufficient guide in the Bible and his own conscience. In one
sense the distinction between the secular and the religious

life vanished. Monasticism was, so to speak, secularised; all men stood henceforward on the same footing towards God; and that advance, which contained the germ of all subsequent revolutions was so enormous that all else seems insignificant. In another sense, the distinction became more profound than ever before. For, though all might be sanctified, it was their inner life alone which would partake of sanctification. The world was divided into good and evil, light and darkness, spirit and matter. The division between them was absolute; no human effort could span the chasm.

With this break up of Holy Church, further justified by the devastating logic of Calvin, it is small wonder that architecture seemed muddled and uncertain, and that decoration frequently became mistaken for it. Men's buildings very clearly reflect their mental outlook and their social life. Social power had shifted from the Church into secular hands. It is safe to say that, starting with Henry VIII, architecture in this country shifted into the hands of the upper classes. For that reason creative effort was mostly expended in domestic work, the churches that were built took on either a domestic or severely Protestant character, and the face of England changed from remote and ill-connected clusters of magnificent Gothic buildings and squalid Gothic cottages to park-like scenery and stately mansions, connected by roads more frequently used than before. The squalid cottages remained, for, although the social power had shifted, the social order was still much the same. Elderly architectural opinion today divides into two at this point. There are those who admit that no English architecture exists after Henry VII's Chapel. There are those who admit that no English architecture is worth consideration before Inigo Jones. The intermediate period has received a deal of study. The first school of thought look for the Gothic struggling through the decoration, and the second look for the decoration struggling into a classical form.

The style in which the Gothic predominates may be called, inaccurately enough, Elizabethan, and the style in which the classical predominates over the Gothic, equally inaccurately, may be called Jacobean. To save the time of those who do not wish to distinguish between these periods of architectural uncertainty, I will henceforward use the term 'Jacobethan'.

To the outside world the only claim of Jacobethan architecture to consideration is that it is 'antique'. Unfortunately the 'antique' claim is a strong one. To anyone who seriously considers proportion, the top-heavy pediments and awkward goddesses, neither classic nor Gothic, the unshapely curves of a pseudo-classicism will be nothing but unpleasant. Consider such famous transitional mansions as Burghley House or Kirby or Audley End. The fine big windows recall the last glories of Perpendicular churches. But look at the attic. Rows of columns, plastered against a purely ornamental curved gable, rise tier upon tier. The effect is that of a Victorian mahogany overmantel in stone. One longs to fill in the few undecorated spaces that are left with pieces of looking-glass. To me the appeal of Jacobethan is indeed remote. The colouring is sometimes cheerful and harmonious, as may still be seen in some of

the tombs of country churches. But more often the effect of a
building, or of panelling, or of a tomb of this time is vulgar
and ostentatious. Admittedly the work of Torrigiano in Henry
VII's Chapel in Westminster Abbey is an exception. Jacobethan architecture is the product of adventurers who were
more interested in the new-found thrill of money than in
architecture and whose art therefore expressed a care-free,
purse-proud state of mind. This style is saved from the complete atrophy of English architecture today by the fact that
then a man was capable of being care-free and purse-proud at
the same time. Jacobethan architecture may be ugly, but it is
never dull.

The mental upheaval of the immediate post-Reformation
period was a stimulus to literature, but not to architecture. The
extravagance by which it was characterised looked well enough
in the jewelled writings of the Elizabethans, though it required
a genius to set it in order. Such happy truculence could not be
expressed in brick or wood or stone. Under Edward VI, Pro-
tector Somerset made an attempt to establish Calvinism, which
was reversed by Mary into an attempt to establish Romanism.
Elizabeth attempted a compromise, and the end was that brilliant and, let us hope, never-to-be-altered compromise, the
English Common Prayer Book. But it may be easy to still the
ruthless logic of Calvanism with a leaven of Arminianism; it
may be simple to sound the deepest fountain of poetical
imagery with the mythology of the ancients and an ancient
form of Christianity as a double inspiration. Architecture will
not admit of a compromise nor of uncertainty; its demands are

as stern and hide-bound as the materials of which it is composed. It needed a genius to adopt the new way of thinking and to apply it to stone. And in architecture the equivalent of Spenser was Inigo Jones and of Shakespeare, Wren.

Reformation was made more significant by an influx of wealth. Marauders and adventurers found themselves saddled with squalid dwellings unsuited to the state which their new-found freedom expected. Even the yeomen were prosperous. The new wealth led to new building, and, considering the smallness of the population of England at the time, the extent of the new building was surprising. I am sure there is not a reader of this book who cannot recall at least half a dozen time-honoured relics of Jacobethan architecture. Almost every other village of any size has a Jacobethan wing to its manor, either edging incongruously out of the Georgian main block, or responsible for the demolition of the Georgian building at the beginning of this century.

Upon re-reading what I have written, I may have been a little unfair to Jacobethan, because I have only considered buildings in the style as an architectural whole. The detail is frequently beautiful. Humble examples of Jacobethan art are pleasanter than grand ones. I can cite as instances the chests of parish churches, the details of tombs and monuments, the old pews as at Inglesham, near Lechlade, and Walpole St Peter, in Norfolk, the panelling of many a Cotswold manor. These show by the beauty of their craftsmanship and their satisfactory proportions that English architecture was not dead, only temporarily moribund in some of her members.

# Chapter V · Educated Architecture

*Near some fair Town I'd have a private Seat*
*Built uniform; not little, nor too great:*
*Better if on a rising Ground it stood;*
*On this side Fields, on that a neighb'ring Wood.*
*It should, within, no other Things contain*
*But what were Useful, Necessary, Plain:*
*Methinks 'tis nauseous, and I'd ne'er endure*
*The needless Pomp of gaudy Furniture.*

John Pomfret, *The Choice*, 1699

The architecture of humanism, a phrase used by every art critic, and learned at the same time as the rest of the art language, which so many writers find useful and which will probably be fostered by the Courtauld Institute of Art, is generally regarded as the architecture of the Renaissance. Gothic builders planned a building first, or added to an older building, and then fitted in the windows afterwards, to suit their comparatively strange ideas of how much light a room should have. The humanist architect, acting on what he had so far learnt from the humanities, planned the façade and its windows first and fitted in the rooms behind afterwards. This difference in technique is generally regarded as the demarcation between the mediaeval architect and the architect of the Renaissance. Such a difference is, of course, a too hard and fast line by which to divide two periods of even so hard and fast a subject as architecture.

There are buildings that are made entirely for their façade in this country and which exhibit little skill in the plan behind; these are generally modern buildings put up in the Queen Anne manner in London and the provinces. Such work also existed in the eighteenth century, and, although there was not then the coarseness of treatment which we see today in those ghastly white Portland stone edifices of, say, the new Regent Street, they have only the charm of bric-à-brac, rather amusing little things for interior decorators to chat about to clients. Blenheim Palace, though delightful in general grouping, is not more than a piece of gigantic bric-à-brac. This was realised by those sensible people of the eighteenth century, for a contemporary wrote of it:

> See sir, here's the grand approach ;
> This way is for His Grace's coach :
> There lies the bridge, and here's the clock,
> Observe the lion and the cock,
> The spacious court, the colonnade,
> And mark how wide the wall is made !
> The chimneys are so well design'd,
> They never smoke in any wind.
> This gallery's contrived for walking,
> The windows to retire and talk in ;
> The council chamber for debate,
> And all the rest are rooms of state.
>     Thanks sir, cried I, 'tis very fine,
> But where d'ye sleep, or where d'ye dine?
> I find, by all you have been telling
> That 'tis a house, but not a dwelling.

Sir John Vanbrugh, who built it, would have been, had he
lived today, an interior decorator to the very rich. In the
eighteenth century there was no such thing. Men were either
architects or artists. Sir John Vanbrugh was a genius, but
wholly neither. His other enormous building, Castle Howard,
is no wit as imposing as Hawksmoor's comparatively small
mausoleum which stands in its grounds. Hawksmoor wrapped
his life in an industrious obscurity. Though it would be hard to
believe that Vanbrugh, who also wrote plays, was idle.

It should not be hard to tell a building which has been built
purely for effect from one that has been built largely from convenience. The one fails to satisfy after close scrutiny. The
second grows on one, although it may not strike the eye at
first. Few people bother to look at Chelsea Hospital, London,
which I regard as Wren's masterpiece. There it stands, a stately
unadorned brick building, whose north walls are only relieved
by high round-headed windows, the whole façade split in two
by a noble attached portico, behind whose pediment rises one
of those stone cupolas that only Wren perfected, and the
'thirty-nine' buses shift a few indifferent Londoners past it
every day. Yet even Carlyle, who was little alive to an appreciation of the visual arts, heaven knows, is said to have remarked:
'I had passed it daily for many years without thinking about it,
and one day I began to reflect that it had always been a pleasure
to me to see it, and I looked at it more attentively and saw that
it was quiet and dignified and the work of a *gentleman*.' Here is
a building that combines convenience of plan with elegance of
dimensions. The Gothic tradition was not dead. It did not

even sleep. It was translated into humanism. No one could say that all Wren's city churches were Renaissance buildings. Who saw an ancient Roman edifice which had even a detail like any part of the soaring steeple of St Bride's Church in Fleet Street?

And not only did the Gothic tradition go on in the larger public buildings of the late seventeenth and throughout the eighteenth century, but also in domestic architecture. An upper class ruled the country and acquired a dignity suitable to its office. The eighteenth century has been interpreted by the fanciful performances of the Lyric Theatre, Hammersmith, as an age of Ombre and 'Obleegement' and a quaint old-world artiness that has already descended to the higher-class tea-shops. Edmund Dulac, Lovat Fraser and their countless imitators have sentimentalised a hard, reasonable age, which produced a hard and reasonable architecture—buildings which were described in Victorian guide books as 'barrack-like' mansions, but which contained behind their nobly proportioned façades a plan fitting in reasonably and well with the social plan of their age. There would be the spacious entrance hall with possibly a ceiling of elaborated plaster-work, while an imposing staircase, with heavily wrought iron or carved wood balusters, formed the main feature of it, and terminated in a gallery leading to the bedrooms. Meanwhile, on the ground floor, double doors with moulded architraves led to saloons, and thence to drawing-rooms and libraries, the one leading out of the other, for all Georgian rooms contain two entrances. Nor would the magnificence of the entrance be confined to their mouldings and their

proportions. The architect would design furniture and adorn-
ments to fit his rooms; and, although there are few examples
of this splendid tradition left in England today, there are still
many houses of Ireland, where the Victorian sunlight flooded
in less gaudily, that possess their ancient fittings. I have seen
many late Georgian houses in Ireland whose severe mahogany
furniture remains in the niches designed for it, whose porcelain
and silver is of the eighteenth century, whose wallpaper is
Chinese, put up when the house was built, houses where even
the contemporary fenders and pokers have remained. The inhabitants were eighteenth-century characters too.

Perhaps the first idea of what the eighteenth century was like,
as well as of what the mediaeval was like, may be gained by the
Englishman by a visit to Ireland. For that country, as George
Moore has said, was never subjected to a nineteenth century.
It has fortunately escaped the industrialism which changed the
face of England, if it had not yet changed her architectural
vision, and there are still but two classes of any importance—
the peasant and the landlord. Admittedly the Land Acts have
deprived the last of his powers, but he still hangs on, eccentric
and splendid in his (s)mouldering Georgian mansion.

As late as 1870 it was possible for Adolphus Cooke, of
Cookesborough, to annoy the foxhunting gentlemen of Westmeath by keeping two half-wits, whose opinion he consulted
on his every act, and to amaze his workmen by ordering them
to pick up the twigs off his lawn and build nests for the rooks.
Such eccentricity would not have been countenanced in many
other parts of Europe at the time. Should a man wish to live

in the eighteenth century, let him take with him what capital he has left, and buy one of those hundreds of empty Georgian mansions in the remote parts of Ireland. There, with his undulating park around him, the railway far distant and never the sound of a motor car near, he may drink himself to an honourable death, keeping his individuality alive.

Though he may have been a despot, the eighteenth-century landlord was not often the fop that he has been pictured by lovers of the antique today. The typical relations between patron and architect are illustrated in these letters between Lord Ongley, newly created in the peerage of Ireland, and Batty Langley, Architect. Langley was famous in his day for his practical books on mouldings, chimney-pieces, grottoes, doors, windows, useful at once to the man of taste and to the builder. His one venture in experimentalism crowned him with ridicule, for he attempted to divide Gothic architecture into five orders. The book in which he put forward this theory was instrumental in reviving an interest in that style, whose dire consequences will be seen later on. These letters, which I have the pleasure of printing below, show the relations between patron and architect:

To Batty Langley, Esq.,
        Archt.
    Lord Ongley presents his compliments and is obliged to Mr. Langley for his designs for his new residence at Old Warden. He was insistent, when he last saw Mr. Langley, on all absence of *Fandango* and of plaster-work within the

house in the saloons and withdrawing-rooms, in what it pleases Mr. Langley to call the *Gothick* or *Hermit* style. Vitruvius, as Mr. Langley is no doubt aware, says that architecture consists of *Fabric et ratiocinatio*. If Mr. Langley will allow the latter of these two qualities to exercise his mind he will know that neither Lord Ongley nor Lady Ongley are Goths or Hermits. Though they would not wish their entertainments to be ostentatious, they would wish them to be profuse. Mr. Langley has provided no more than two withdrawing-rooms from the saloon, nor has he provided the space necessary for his Lordship's collection of ancient coins and busts. The library is not large enough and the accommodation for Lord Ongley's servants, who number twenty-six, though fitting for their station, it can but be obvious to Mr. Langley, is inadequate for the storing and cooking requisite for the banquets that are projected in the New Hall at Old Warden. Should Mr. Langley desire further to display his skill in abstruse and *ancient* styles, Lord Ongley will be pleased for him to do so in the *Summer Pavilion* and *Eyecatchers*. Considerable acreage of land in the county is in the possession of Lord Ongley, and the eminence on which the New Hall is to be situate commands a fine prospect as far as Langford and Clifton Arlesey, all of which can be cleared to widen up the view and cause Lord Ongley's mansion and domain to be another Chatsworth, Carton or a Russborough. Mr. Langley will save his Lordship considerable time in writing lengthy letters, if he will send a larger design with a bolder frontage and a finer and *less mean* interior, worthy both of his Lordship's rank in life and the talents of his architect. Should this be impossible there is doubtless another *modern Vitruvius* capable of producing a design worthier of Lord Ongley's patronage than is Mr. Langley.

*Sept.* 17, 1770.

Old Warden, Bedfordshire.


*Mr Langley's Answer*

MY LORD,

I am in no way to be thought to despise or to take into little account the gracious condescension which your Lordship has hitherto seen fit to employ. But, my Lord, there is a moment when plain words must be uttered. I have spent near thirty year now in the prosecution of my business of architect and with great toil and application I have arrived at a proper estimation, or so I would believe, of what is due both to your Lordship and to your humble servant. I grant the truth of your Lordship's observations as to the withdrawing-rooms, and the space needed for your Lordship's collections; and these matters, as that of due provision for the storage of victuals and the cooking and serving of the same, shall be speedily amended, should your Lordship see fit to continue his present patronage. On all these matters, I bow to your Lordship's greater knowledge and cry *Mea Culpa!*

But, my Lord, though I admit the truth of Vitruvius his observation, which your Lordship cites, I see not the application. My bosom almost bursts when I read your Lordship, so justly renowned for his learning and taste, to despise the *Gothick* or *Hermit* manner. My Lord, bethink you, if I may make so bold, that we have cast aside this two years the fashions which your Lordship would prefer; that *Fandango* and *Gothick* plasterwork *within* are now universal in the politest circles.

Your humble servant's station in life is so far below that of your Lordship, that only the sternest necessity would lead him to address your Lordship in such bold terms. But, my Lord, I should not be an honest man, nor deserving of your Lordship's regard, were I not to say plainly that what your Lordship would desire is *out of fashion*, and that *Fandango* is *in*. Of the truth of this I have the strongest assurance from the metropolis so late as last Thursday week.

I pray you, my Lord, give further consideration to the matter. I study only your Lordship's interests when I say that I cannot bring myself to confine the *Gothick* to the purlieus of your new Mansion. The whole must be of a piece and in consonance. My conscience will not allow me to play *hoity-toity* with so serious a matter.

I fear I shall have offended your Lordship in daring thus to express myself, but believe me, my Lord, nothing is further from the thoughts of your humble servant than to offend his most esteemed and worshipful patron.

I am, my Lord,

Your Lordship's humble servant,

BATTY LANGLEY.

## Lord Ongley to Batty Langley

Mr. Langley, do not speak to me about the fashions for what I know of them I despise and what I do not I prefer to ignore. I asked for a noble palace and all I receive is ignoble flattery. Were you as able with your pencil as you are with your quill I would have more words of commendation for designs which I doubt I will ever receive. It is eight weeks now since I returned to you your former plans as mean conceptions, overloaded with decoration, since then I have had no more than your polite but indefinite letter. Allow me, sir, to state my wants and if my temper seems to get the better of me, remember that it is through stating my wants too often, both to you in person and through the tiresome medium of a written statement. I require a mansion worthy of the position I occupy with regard to my tenantry, and worthy of the landskip in which I have chosen to place it. First let it be convenient, next let it be elegant without ostentation, impressive without Italian or Gothick heaviness, desirable without exciting the envy of the covetous, yet calculated to impress the mean-spirited. All these qualities it is possible for an architect to incorporate in his designs if he is not so guided by fashion that he cannot call his soul the possession of an All Wise Creator, and if he is not so lacking in the Spirit of Inspiration that he cannot conceive greater grandeur than he sees from his window in St. Giles. Sir Christopher Wren and Mr. Gibbs, and even my lamented father's friend Dean Aldrich, were capable of fine conceptions and of carrying them out honestly and without undue expense. You have the reputation they enjoyed, let me see their ability. As for your ideas of fashion let them be guided by *ratiocinatio*. Doubtless your Goths and Hermits will be welcomed by empty headed cits who have neither the Learning nor the Breeding to find worthier objects of entertainment. I do not wish to dispose the patronage which you have enjoyed from yourself to someone of more rapid methods. Pray let me have the plans with due haste; my Lady Ongley wilts in her present discomfort here, since it is not the time to go to Bath while I regret the rude shelter which my ancestors enjoyed, as my mind daily awaits the spacious dwelling you are to prepare, and is daily disappointed.

ONGLEY.

We notice in these letters Lord Ongley's sourness over the new *Gothick Fandango* which Batty Langley, above all people, would be most anxious to provide. Lord Ongley had the ruling hand and, like the majority of his class at that time, he preferred to let state and dignity overrule mere fashions in taste.

It must strike the foreigner as curious that, when English architectural styles become what old-fashioned purists will call 'debased', they become simpler. That 'debased' style, Perpendicular Gothic, and its even more 'debased' Tudor successor went in the opposite direction to architecture abroad. In England any buildings containing 'flamboyant' features, similar to the late Gothic periods in France and Germany, can be counted on one hand. Where Continental architects branched

off into a morass of decoration for decoration's sake, as in
many hideous hôtels de villes in Flanders and prickly cathedrals, English architecture seemed to be shorn of all superfluities. It is a long cry from the austerity of fifteenth century
buildings like King's College Chapel to contemporary edifices
abroad.

So with the eighteenth century we find an even greater restraint practised in England. There was hardly any *Rococo*.
Among the only examples of *Rococo* decoration in England are
those large gilt Chippendale glasses in the Chinese or the
French manner, which so frequently form the only elaborate
feature of the English withdrawing-room. Here and there an
essay in the Chinese taste, either in a cabinet for the house or in
a bridge or grotto near some undulation of the park, marked the
only excursion of the English gentleman from his true tradition. Our aristocracy, when it controlled the public taste, was
too serious and politically and logically minded to indulge in
any artistic hobbies outside antiquarianism. And if there was
any *Rococo* in this country, it did not express itself in those acres
of tinted plasterwork, those trumpeting cherubim and long-
drawn perspectives with which the Sitwells have made us
familiar, but in sham ruins, sham keeps, pseudo-Gothic abbeys
and romantic plaster castles, that grew so sophisticated as the
eighteenth century wore into the nineteenth, as to be mistaken
for the very objects they travestied. Classical architecture, having cast off decorative impulse, depended more and more on
proportion. A style was created more lovely than any European
architecture; the crescents and squares of Bath; the crescent at

Buxton; and in every considerable town, well-proportioned
assembly rooms, plain without, decorously arrayed by the
Brothers Adam within. Decoration became flatter and flatter,
until it sank into the building and scarcely dared show itself
outside the house. Who would think, walking down Henrietta
Street, Dublin,* or enjoying the ever-opening vistas in Mer-
rion Square, that the delicate fanlight over a modest front door
in a plain red brick house was a token of the carved balusters,
plaster ceilings emblazoned with medallions, and marble
mantelpieces within? Who, walking down Wimpole Street or
Harley Street today, attempting down those endless perspectives to find his doctor, would expect to see the magnificent
staircase behind the front door? And, should his doctor have
left his waiting-room un-Jacobethanised, would he not be surprised at the splendid proportions and marble mantel which
confront him? Nor are these interiors in any sense *Rococo*; they
are not extravagant, the beauty of the effect is in the tiny
mould of a cornice or the delicate flattened urn on a mantel.

I do not wish to say there is no *Baroque* or *Rococo* in England.
(I am taking these words to mean 'extravagant', wrongly perhaps, but the differences between them and the wideness of the
terms need not be discussed here, and for that reason I may do
devotees of *Baroque* and *Rococo* an unwitting injustice.) Blenheim Palace, much of the interior of Wilton House, the town of
Blandford Forum, Greenwich Hospital, the Rotunda Hospital
Chapel, Dublin, and State rooms in various palaces and town
halls are in the accepted *Baroque*, and very fine they are. But
* Now demolished.

for the most part English classical architecture simplified itself just as Gothic did, and behaved in the contrary way to Continental styles. We have only to visit the Wallace Collection or a Mayfair-Italianate antique dealer to see the various styles that were prevalent in the rest of Europe.

Everyone can tell an eighteenth-century house if he uses his eyes. The material is generally local brick or stone; the front of the house is flat, and the windows, whose shape is made interesting by the sizes of the panes divided by thick glazing bars in earlier, and thin in later examples, are smaller on the first floor than on the ground floor and smaller still on the top floor. The roof is generally hidden by a low wall or balustrade, and the servants' bedrooms looked out on to this brick parapet, or possibly on to a balustrade which served the purpose of a plain parapet in earlier houses. Servants, when there were only two classes, lived 'according to their station'. The outbuildings of an eighteenth-century house are always well proportioned, and all roofs at this time were made with tiles larger at the bottom, going smaller as they reached the ridge at the top. Any decorative extravagance confined itself to the front door of the house, which perhaps had the familiar pediment over it, or a round head containing a lead fanlight. If the house did not face flat on the street, keeping an orderly, dignified countenance next its neighbours of whatever style, a neat wrought-iron gate broke the high brick wall which kept the continuity of the street. Houses like these exist in every large town today of any antiquity. They even exist in West Ham and Walthamstow. They are so unpretentious that commercial gentlemen like to pull them down or cover their undecorated surfaces with advertisements or plate glass windows. It is only when these houses have been done away with that people realise how pleasant such buildings were. In many country towns they still exist untouched, generally occupied by solicitors or doctors or retired soldiers' widows, who look out on to the street through broad curtains, regretting their horse-drawn pasts.

Yet these simple buildings of the eighteenth century are not things over which we should sentimentalise. They are for the most part inconvenient for modern conditions, where servants and householders are more or less on an equality. They were built with boldness in their time, to suit the people for whom their many anonymous artists designed them. Because they were built with boldness and sincerity, because they were fit for their purpose, they harmonised with any Tudor and mediaeval buildings surrounding them. It is sentimental and silly to build in their style now, though it may not be sentimental to copy their severity and the restful lines of their cornices. No eighteenth-century architect would have countenanced the imitation of his style today. The man who had the courage to place the great round classical dome of the Radcliffe Camera, hemmed in on every side by Gothic fronts and towers and spires, and by reason of his courage to make that dome the pivot of the University of Oxford, would also have had the courage to build today as sincere an essay in modern materials in its place.* Such courage is the genius of architecture; it is

* Fallacious. I suppose this is the only excuse Colonel Seifert can make for Centre Point, Tottenham Court Road.

neither classical nor Gothic; it is merely an expression of its age. Therefore the visitor to Oxford need not be surprised by the products of our own age's architecture in the University buildings—feeble imitations of styles of the past. For when we contemplate that glorious English eighteenth century, we feel that England as an architectural influence is finished.

Why was England an abiding and a restraining influence in architecture? Why did the style of architecture in palace, town house, country mansion, farmhouse, church, chapel and row of workmen's cottages simplify itself instead of bursting into Continental exuberance? England was rich. She was peaceful. She was agricultural.

I think the reasons for this simplicity are two; in the first place, England had finished her social revolution before the eighteenth century had begun. The battle between Cavaliers and Roundheads, and the partial reform of the Parliamentary system forbade the existence of an aristocracy totally uninterested in politics, only interested in pleasure and the arts. France was to pay for her *Rococo*: so were Italy, Germany, Austria, Spain and the rest of Europe. The educated ruled, but could not tyrannise. Cowper expressed the popular sentiment in 'The Task', though, like all popular sentiments, his contained but a shadow of the truth. 'Slaves cannot breathe in England', and English eighteenth-century architecture is the expression of the serious-minded, reasonable few who controlled it, divided by Theism and Atheism, Antinomianism and Calvinism, and lashed for their faults by Pope and Swift and Churchill.

And what the Commonwealth did not do for the solving of the upper classes and their architecture, the Methodist Revival finished off. Not only did it cause Lady Huntingdon to think twice about employing Angelica Kaufmann to paint the ceilings of her house, but it also prevented merchants, mayors, corn chandlers and bankers from parading their growing wealth in ostentatious buildings.

In fact, the reasoned Protestantism of England in the eighteenth century, of an age not so much of faith as of Sovereign Grace, was largely responsible for the simplicity of its architure. The Quakers, the Baptists, the Independents, the Unitarians, the Presbyterians, whose humble brick meeting-houses, survivals of Commonwealth days, lie hidden away from persecution, deep in the back streets of many country towns and in the remoter hamlets from Somerset to Yorkshire, were a chastening influence. Then came John Wesley, saying that all could be saved, and that in 'My father's house are many mansions'; and Whitefield preaching that God had prepared a house for them; what need was there of a carved stone dwelling in the high street, of a gilded saloon, of grottoes in the garden, if heaven was built with jasper bulwarks and its streets were paved with gold? 'Lay not up for yourselves treasure upon earth.' Such a message as this completed the work that Cromwell had started. And its influence still survives in that day of rest, the English Sunday.

Today the Lord's Day Observance Society, which takes such exception to American films of American luxury on the Sabbath, has become the object of ridicule with those who spin

down in their super sports cars along the main road to a replica
of London at Maidenhead or Brighton; it is probably ridiculed
by architects who can afford a motor car.

Yet there are still places where one can appreciate the English Sunday; where the architecture shows up in the silent
streets, and the glamour of the shops is for the moment shut-
tered, and the loud speaker is silenced in the wireless depot.
Imagine yourself in Portsmouth on a Lord's Day morning.
Portsmouth is associated with Evangelicalism, a form of religion which seems to grip men who have retired from the navy.
The bells are pealing all over the town. Heavy music from the
Cathedral church, whose Portland stone tower rides splendidly
over the red brick High Street; a tenor bell calls insistently to
Holy Eucharist at St Michael's—an 1880 imitation of a
mediaeval church; a tenor bell calls less insistently to Matins at
St George's. St George's was a pleasant church once, built in
the reign of George III, a square brick building, condemned by
the superficial as 'too plain', and consequently 'Gothicised'.
The galleries were disfigured, the box pews cut down, the
windows filled with that repulsive material known as 'Cathedral
Glass', which sheds a pale pink or pale green light the
colour of Bible atlases, and therefore, I suppose, religious; St
George's is a wreck. But least insistent of all the bells on a
Lord's Day morning, that sound across the narrow streets and
over a placid harbour and silent dockyard, is the bell that calls
to Morning Prayer at St John's, Portsea. 'High St Michael's',
'Poor St George's,' 'Low St John's' they say in Portsmouth,
and St John's is the last eighteenth-century church that re-

mains totally unspoiled,* which I know of in England. For even the service is eighteenth century. And it is there that we will go to worship this morning.

You would hardly notice the church, so well does it fit in with the street, a red brick building, the lines of whose windows do not disturb the houses, which continue in unbroken rows on either side. The doors are apart, and when we have pushed open that of the paned glass screen which leads from the vestibule to the church, what a sight meets the gaze! A forest of woodwork, of excellent joinery; round the walls above, tier the empty galleries, with hard but seemly seats for poorer people, below and level with our shoulders the box pews for the gentry, with their doors which shut with a loud smack. High above the pews is the double-deck pulpit with the clerk's desk beneath. And at the end of the church the holy table, carefully removed from the wall so as to conform with Protestant doctrine, encircled by simple communion rails. Look up at the white plaster ceiling pleasantly moulded. The incumbent enters. He is wearing the black gown, just as his predecessor of 150 years ago. The congregation, which can only be seen when it stands above its grained oak fastness, is small and bleak. But the rich and scented, who occupied those fine pews when the church was built, have left Portsea, and now their descendants live in half-timbered detached residences which their parents built in the more refined and remoter suburbs.

And at the same time that the bells are ringing for service, there are some places of worship from which no bells call. A

* It was bombed by the Germans in World War II, and totally destroyed.

stucco Congregational Chapel in a solid Greek manner of 1825, a Wesleyan Chapel in terra cotta Gothic, riddled with dedication stones bearing the date 1888, and many another fane of some odd denomination in pious but bastard Gothic—all stand with their doors open and churchwardens or elders waiting to show us to our seats.

Do not despise the English Sunday. When it is gone, like the elegant terrace or the simple brick house in the High Street, it will be missed. Sunday is sacred to Protestantism, and Protestantism purified our architecture. Now the machine has set the pace, and a month of Sundays will not slow it down.

# Chapter VI · Regency Architecture

## The Educated Classes State-Conscious

*Suburban villas, highway side retreats,*
*That dread the encroachment of our growing streets,*
*Tight boxes neatly sash'd, and in a blaze*
*With all a July sun's collected rays,*
*Delight the citizen, who, gasping there,*
*Breathes clouds of dust, and calls it country air.*

William Cowper, *Retirement*

In the present age when the pride of possession is a curse, taxed by the State and envied by the people, I retain it in one matter, that of books. And among all my books those I most like examining, the elegance of whose prefatory remarks is even surpassed by the beauty of their coloured illustrations, are my aquatinted books which date from 1800 to 1830. Not only the coloured Rowlandsons depicting the Tour of Doctor Syntax in Search of The Picturesque, not only illustrated tours of the Grand Junction Canal, not only graceful depictions of contemporary modes and rural life, but also the folio publications of architects, illustrating gentlemen's residences, improvements in landskip gardening, suggestions for summer pavilions or for cottages for the labouring classes, delight me. There is no end to such books, and I can safely say that not one of the many hundreds I have seen and longed to buy has been devoid of merit.

Oh, happy days of the Regency, when the learned had schooled themselves into an outward semblance of responsibility to set an example to rising industrialists, though they might reflect the glitter of the Regent in their hearts; happy days when Shelley and Wordsworth, when Byron and Keats and Hood and Hunt sang among the whirr of the wheels of industry that were to roll Britannia in a chariot to Progress; in days like these my books were different from their counterparts of fifty years before; the flourishes had disappeared from their title pages, the subservience from their dedications; their margins had broadened and their type had been simplified; Bodoni had taken the place of Baskerville, decoration had yielded to space. And as in the typography of books, so had the houses of the Regency been simplified. 'To be natural and unaffected is the first rule of good taste,' wrote Edmund Aikin, an obscure provincial architect in 1810. The houses had indeed become simplified, so strictly utilitarian, so decent, that there exist portfolios of architectural examples, published a little over 100 years ago, which may be compared with contemporary domestic architecture in Germany, where the wall surfaces are large and the windows small and regular, and the houses gain an effect therefrom in no way to be associated with antiquity.

Perhaps the best impression of the Regency outlook, of that simplicity which was the logical outcome of the Greek revival, which succeeded the Roman revival of the middle of the eighteenth century, may best be obtained from typical contemporary pronouncements.

In 1810 Mr Edmund Aikin, an architect who will only be

known now by those who have bothered to look at the Wellington Assembly Rooms, Liverpool, published a book of designs for villas and other rural buildings, engraved on thirty-one plates with plans and explanations, together with an introductory essay. From the introductory essay, written in an elegant style, the reader may be entertained, even startled, by extracts. Aikin was a typical architect of his period, trained for architecture when Messrs Stewart and Revett had just published their drawings of Grecian antiquities. He and his elders fell under the spell of the Greek revival in architecture, and in their enthusiasm threw off the old school of architects who went for their models to ancient Rome. The day of the long façade of engaged columns, the 'original steeple', the Italian window, the rusticated lower storeys, the circular temple on the mound in the park, the red brick with stone dressings and heavy key-stones over door and window depicting old men's faces, the day of the houses that M. R. James describes so well, the day even of white Portland stone and the imitation of the manner of Wren and his noble contemporaries, the delicate and flattened patterns of the Italian school was over. Greek architecture brought in simplicity. It checked any tendency to the *Rococo* of the Continent; and that style had to be content with comparative obscurity. It appears sometimes in the corners of clock faces, on Cotswold tombstones, where there was no Flaxman and no Bacon to influence the carver, and in confectionery, where it remains in wedding-cake designs, and on those pink, white and green cakes which are known in teashops as 'pastries'. It has also survived in fairs.

But Aikin, like his talented contemporaries, discovered that the Greek style was not enough. You could not go on reproducing the Parthenon or the Erechtheum. You could not even take the details, as early Renaissance architects had taken Roman details, alter their proportions and set them up, now as the ornamentation over a mantel, now as a pleasing innovation on a façade, now as a steeple. They had no Jacobethan period of experiment in the change of style from Roman to Greek, such as Renaissance architects had in changing from Gothic to Italian. They were open to hard logic.* When the Jacobethans had experimented in brick and stone, the effect had not always come off; the Greek revivalists reasoned before building. They thought about construction, and realised that detail was of small moment, and that on construction and proportion depended effect. Of course, this had been realised before, but not so widely. Nor had it been carried so far to its logical conclusions, except in 'utilitarian' buildings like barns, meeting-houses and farms, which remained as truly Gothic as they had always been and as Regency architecture subsequently became.

Hear the words of Edmund Aikin, the typical Regency architect, who expired after a painful struggle at his father's house at Stoke Newington, on March 11th, 1820. This is what he wrote ten years before his death in the introductory essay I have already mentioned:

The style of modern Architecture is universally admitted to be founded upon what is called the antique, which has

* About which I didn't then know anything, and still know nothing.

been praised with blind admiration, and acknowledged as authority, in a manner to preclude the exercise of rational criticism: but it may be doubted whether this admiration has been as sincere as vehement, and has not been confined to words and theory, instead of guiding practice. In fact, it may be asserted, with the most trifling exceptions, that no modern building could ever be mistaken for an ancient edifice, setting aside all adventitious marks and dates, and considering each architecturally, or as represented in a drawing. To what can this essential difference be owing? Modern Architects profess to imitate antique examples, and do so in columns, entablatures, and details, but never in the general effect. Is it that they imitate blindly, and without penetrating into those principles and that system, which is superior to the details and guides them? This is a subject which it may be useful and interesting to pursue.

Whoever examines the remains of Grecian Architecture, must be struck with the extreme simplicity of their construction: parallelograms, surrounded with or enclosing ranges of columns, are nearly all that he will meet with. The system of decoration is not separated from that of construction, but forms an essential part of it. The wooden hut is the model of both, the post and lintel are transmuted into the column and entablature, and the cabin into a temple. That the earliest Grecian temples were really of wood is rendered probable, from the circumstance of so many of them being burnt during the invasion of Xerxes; and that wood has sometimes been employed as the principal material in erecting large and magnificent edifices, is shown by the example of the Temple of Jerusalem, which was constructed with pillars of cedar. However, in a country like Greece, abounding with stone and marble, these superior materials would soon supersede the use of timber; and this circumstance would effect certain changes in the forms of Architecture. A wooden lintel, from its fibrous texture, possessing considerable tenacity and strength, in proportion to its weight, may be employed in bearings, where a stone architrave would break by its own gravity; accordingly Vitruvius relates, that the Tuscan temples, in which the intercolumniations were very wide, had wooden architraves. When, therefore, porticoes were erected of stone, it was necessary, in order to insure solidity, to contract the distance between the columns to very narrow limits. A timber building, never secure from accidents by fire or violence, would seldom be constructed with any great solidity or magnificence; but in stone it is possible, as the energetic industry of the ancient Egyptians has shown, to defy the injuries of time, and almost the violences of rapine. The Architect who builds in stone, may build for eternity; and this idea will offer a motive for that grand solidity of construction, which is an essential element of the sublime in Architecture.

These circumstances led to the perfection of the Grecian style. The original model secured that inestimable simplicity of form and construction which satisfies the judgment, while a superior material preserved it from the meagreness attendant on wooden building, and the hand of

taste crowned the whole with grace and beauty. Thus arose
the Doric, or, as it might be emphatically called, the Grecian
Order, the first-born of Architecture, a composition which
bears the authentic marks of its origin, in the forms of
wooden construction transferred to stone.

The Romans derived their style of Architecture from the
Greeks; but, practising it as imitators, further removed
from the original model, and with less severity of taste, they
formed a style of magnificence and luxury, always grand, but
not unfrequently licentious and incongruous.

The arch was discovered: this is the noblest improvement in the building art; an invention which enables man to
bridle the mighty river, to raise aloft the self-balanced pile,
and cover with the pensile vault the vast area of a temple of
all the Gods. But it may be doubted, whether the arch,
though enlarging the powers of construction, has not, in
fact, been detrimental to Architecture, considered as a fine
art. The system of Grecian Architecture is, as has been
observed, founded upon the principles of wooden construction, but the arch may be said to be the natural style of
stone: the use of the arch therefore introduced a new and
inconsistent principle of imitation, degraded the simplicity
of the original model, and caused a confusion of ideas, of
forms and practices, from which Architecture has never
recovered.

On the revival of arts and letters, in the fourteenth and
fifteenth centuries, Architecture re-appeared in Italy. The
vast remains of Roman magnificence were disinterred from

the ruins and obscurity which had so long covered them, and excited an admiration ardent and enthusiastic. Then was the hand of every artist employed in copying and measuring, and his mind in arranging and systematising. The Orders were discovered, and numerous treatises offered theories and delivered rules for their execution. From Italy the mode spread over the other countries of Europe; the Italians had imitated the Ancients, but other nations imitated them; and in every country arose ambitious rivals of Italian villas and cathedrals. The Architecture of the Middle Ages was branded with the appellation of Gothic, and condemned to an indiscriminating contempt, which only in our own country, and in our own times, has been dispelled.

The comparison of ancient and modern Architecture will rather present contrasts than resemblances, although the latter professes to be the disciple and follower of the former. In the remains of ancient edifices, the greatest simplicity, and even uniformity, prevails in the general plans and dispositions, and an infinite variety in the details; so that it would perhaps be impossible to find any two examples of an Order precisely similar in proportions, forms, and ornaments. At the same time, this exuberant fancy is so well restrained within reasonable limits, that the whole collection of columns, with very slight exceptions, may be resolved into three characteristic Orders, the Doric, the Ionic, and the Corinthian. Possessing three expressions, the strong, the elegant, and the rich, the Ancients knew that it was all that Architecture could say distinctly, and any attempt to enlarge would but weaken and confuse her language. The details were committed to the fancy or taste of the individual artist, but the general dispositions appear to have been determined by rules, which none dared or wished to violate.

Modern Architects, on the other hand, while they permit themselves a boundless license in the general plans and forms of buildings, have attempted to fix inviolably the proportions of the Orders; each artist recommending such as his peculiar studies have caused to make a favourable impression on his mind, either attempting to average the varieties of ancient models, or fixing on some one example for a standard; as if to change a moulding or ornament were a capital crime against Architecture.

The Gothic style of Architecture, though decried and condemned in words, has exerted a secret and powerful influence on the forms of modern buildings. Hence the affection of extraordinary height, hence the multiplicity of parts, of projections, of angles. Steeples are wholly of Gothic origin; and it may be confidently asserted, that the generality of modern churches, though dressed with columns, entablatures, pediments, and other members belonging to antique architecture, have really a much greater affinity to Gothic building.

Columns were regarded as a necessary decoration to every building which had any pretensions to beauty or magnificence; but, no longer suffered to form colonnades, they were generally engaged in a wall; and thus, deprived of all use, the column was degraded to an idle and ostentatious ornament. This may be regarded as the prominent and capital fault of modern Architecture. . . . The plain and evident use of columns is to form porticoes, ambulatories covered at the top and open at the sides; exactly the kind of walks that warm climates require, which, while they shelter from the sun and rain, leave a free passage to the air; and this destination is pointed out by every ancient edifice. Who would build a colonnade for the purpose of walling it up? Then what folly to produce that appearance, by attaching half columns to a wall!

\*　　　\*　　　\*

The pediment is an important and original member of Grecian Architecture: it is the gable end of a roof, and thus considered, its origin will point out its proper use and application. But in modern buildings the pediment is generally employed as a mere decoration, and has undergone the most ridiculous transformations.

But it is not my intention to go through all the abuses of modern Architecture; those already mentioned are sufficient, for the present purpose, to show that the antique style has never been revived or understood, and that modern Architecture is by no means the imitator of the former. These abuses belong not to accessories, but to essentials; they affect not the details, but the whole system and theory of the art: but they are the practices of the greatest names in modern art, abuses which form their style, and upon which their reputation is built.

The age of invention is gone by, and that of criticism has succeeded: it remains for us, if we cannot rival the beauties of our predecessors, to avoid their defects; to apply with judgment, if we cannot invent with genius; and to follow the guidance of just system, if we cannot track the flights of imagination. Every style of Architecture lies open to our choice, and there is no *prima facie* reason why one should be preferred to another. Any mode may be adopted with reason, but none without. . . . No one can apply justly, who does not penetrate the system and theory upon which any style of Architecture is founded; but possessing this, he will not copy but imitate; he will be able to modify the style adopted to suit the required purpose, and, while altering details or proportions, to preserve character and system.

*          *          *

The attempt to produce a deception in building is absurd, and productive of disappointment. An English villa can be neither a castle, nor an abbey, nor a temple; and even though at a distance, and at first sight, the resemblance may deceive, that nearer inspection which detects the imposture is sure to punish it with contempt and ridicule. Those very feelings, which most powerfully operate to excite pleasure in beholding a genuine remain of antiquity, will have a contrary effect towards a recent imitation. What observer, after catching a view of a turret embowered in wood, and approaching, in expectation of beholding an ancient castle, would not feel a sensible mortification on finding a modern villa? But the builder of modern Gothic is naturally led to attempt deception; for, in considering Gothic Architecture, we never generalize the style and reduce it to elements capable of application to all kinds of edifices, like the Grecian, but we think of particular buildings, of castle, abbeys, or cathedrals, and thus any person attempting to build in the Gothic style, will be in a manner compelled to imitate one of these species of buildings.

*         *         *

The advice given to translators will apply to the Architect: he must endeavour to think like an Ancient placed in modern times, avoiding equally the servility of frigid copying, and the license of incongruous alteration.

The builder of a modern villa has nothing to do with systyle or eustyle intercolumniations; let these particulars be guided by the requisites of internal convenience: neither is it necessary to adhere to any particular canon of proportions, in shaft, capital, or entablature; these only may be properly and gracefully varied with circumstances; but this rule I would observe with inviolable strictness; to give the column its natural and appropriate employment, to make it a *bonâ fide* support, and never to degrade it to the rank of an idle ornament. Every member belonging to construction

I would retain with the same fidelity, but reserve the liberty
of altering any merely ornamental part as taste might
dictate.

                    *         *         *

The principle of contrast will lead to oppose ornament to
plainness, by which alone decoration acquires its full value
and effect.

                    *         *         *

Variety and contrast sometimes give a charm to buildings
which, considered in detail, are really mean and ugly.

In carrying these principles into execution in the designs
of modern villas, it will be necessary to avoid the contact of
equal parts; to reject the square and the cube, and, thus
escaping monotony, the composition will acquire character
and expression. The elevation should be either broad and
low, or high and narrow, or a combination of both; and, to
descend from the general forms to particulars, a long low
front may be pierced with high narrow openings, and a
lofty tower with broad windows. The general form may be
varied by differences in projection or elevation, or a straight
front may be broken by the shapes and dispositions of the
windows. Paucity and smallness of the openings will give
an expression of strength and solidity, and large and frequent
windows an air of gaiety and cheerfulness. The medium of
these qualities would give no expression at all, and cause that
insipidity which is most carefully to be avoided. They may,
however, be introduced in different parts of the same

building, and, being kept quite distinct, they will operate, not as interdestructive quantities, but as contrasts to heighten the effect of each other. Of course, the pursuit of variety must be under the guidance of judgment, and kept subordinate to utility, that it may not degenerate into extravagance.

\* \* \*

I have, in almost all the Designs, wholy omitted everything which may be called ornament, wishing their beauty, if they possess any, to depend upon their general forms and proportions, and thus endeavouring to attain an economical style of beauty, to which ornament is neither necessary nor inapplicable.

And examples of work by Aikin and his contemporaries exist all over England today. They are decent stone villas arranged in squares, crescents or terraces; they are so unpretentious that one does not notice their ample painted surfaces, or so magnificent that one takes them for granted, like Park Crescent, Cumberland Terrace, Waterloo Place and Carlton House Terrace in London. I associate them with Sunday afternoon walks in provincial towns. It is then, generally, that one finds a terrace or a crescent, slightly on the outskirts, wedged in between the mediaeval part of the old town, with its winding streets interspersed with towering brick houses of 200 years ago, and the Gothic revival suburbs beyond. Generally the houses are two, or at the most three, storeys high; the stucco is peeling from their once elegant façades; the grass laid out before them is long and rank with weeds; the corner house bears a name in incised letters which have been allowed to become illegible with the decay of the stucco—'Adelaide Terrace', 'Royal Circus', 'York Cottages', 'Hanover Square', 'Brunswick Villas'—names that are memorials to the martyred Hanoverian monarchs, butchered by Thackeray to make a middle-class holiday twenty years later. The houses are inhabited by genteel old invalids, who hobble out of them, black against their stucco Corinthian background, to Baptist, Congregational, Countess of Huntingdon, Reformed Church of England, Brethren, Catholic Apostolic, or Quaker place of worship. The grained oak door shuts with a bang, and a piece of plaster falls from the architrave. But within the empty Sunday house, there is light and plenty. The hall is spacious. To the right, the dining-room looks out on to the terrace, behind it a morning room looks out on to the garden; below, the kitchen clock echoes over the stone floors of the basement. Up the stairs, whose unadorned balusters and slender mahogany rail accentuate the noble sweep of the staircase, the first floor room looks out over the trees to the quiet weed-grown plot of ground in front of the houses, while the folding doors are flung wide. And then from among the gilded furniture, silken hangings, faded samplers and rosewood piano can be seen the full length of the garden, neatly planted with sycamore and ilex, running down between its pale brick walls.

There can be no one without a memory of such a square, or such a row of houses; and, although they are fast being removed as old-fashioned and insanitary, and villas covered with fake half-timbering take their place, there is still hardly a town without its Regency buildings.

Some towns consist almost entirely of Regency and Victorian buildings: Cheltenham, with its noble streets, wide and planted with trees, radiating round its pump room and Pittville Spa; Leamington, with its Jepson Gardens, Clifton, Edinburgh New Town, St John's Wood and Upper Belgravia and parts of Kensington in London, Abercrombie Square in Liverpool—these three last are little towns within a greater—Harrogate, and parts of every cathedral city and town of any antiquity in England.

Next to the simplicity of its architecture and its practicability, the Regency period will always be known for its civic sense. The eighteenth century lavished its abundant genius on a ballroom, a front door, a mansion, a park, or even a single street, but the Regency lavished its genius on whole towns. Bath and Dublin and Buxton are the only eighteenth-century town planning schemes in Great Britain, and mighty triumphs too. But London needed planning. The Duke of Bedford's Estate and the Grosvenor Estate had made various abortive attempts, of which Bedford and Grosvenor Squares and the somewhat gloomy confines of Gower Street were the result. This was in the true eighteenth-century tradition, which lavished adornment on the interior and did not worry as much about street architecture.

But what period of English history except the Regency could have inspired such a scheme as Nash's Regent Street? Even today when we have ruined the proportions of the Quadrant

by building in a pseudo-modern Queen Anne style, when we
have replaced those washable stucco façades with Portland
stone that will grow grey and dull, the former glory remains.
Not even those blind blocks of masonry balanced upon plate
glass plinths pierced with arches, not even the new County
Fire Office, with its flat dome and two chimney stacks like
great ass's ears each side, that shock the eyes of the man
approaching up Lower Regent Street from Waterloo Place,
not even the middle of Piccadilly Circus and the commercial
ostentation of Oxford Circus can take away from the glory of
the scheme. Though now only the curve of Nash's Quadrant
remains, this alone manages to give dignity to the new Regent
Street, though its proportions have been ruined for the sake of
higher buildings and higher rents. But just imagine it when it
was originally started. To the right and left of the steps up to
the Duke of York's Column rises Carlton House Terrace, a
long plaster cliff imposing and solid, set back upon its Doric
stables, given strength and shadow by immense Corinthian
columns. There, Waterloo Place with Decimus Burton's
Athenaeum Club and Barry's two masterpieces beyond it, the
Travellers' and the Reform, harmonising with the street, yet
boldly differing in detail and fenestration: on the right the
United Service Club (now spoiled by a vulgar roof). Then the
whole sloping length of Lower Regent Street with Repton's
Church, and the County Fire Office at the top. Then the
Quadrant in those days adorned with a colonnade. Then block
after block of shops by Soane, Smirke, Nash and all the best
architects of the time. The windows uniform, each displaying

a museum of taste behind well-proportioned oblong panes. The lettering above the shops is uniform, and so the royal march continues past Cockerell's Church to Nash's curious building, All Soul's Church, at the top of Langham Place—a building which perhaps justifies Mr Arthur T. Bolton's sweeping remark, 'the easy theatricalities of Nash'. Then a turn to the left and the broad avenue of Portland Place which ends in Regent's Park. And Regent's Park alone today remains unharmed. At Portland Place the two quadrants of York Crescent burst out to left and right with their mellow colonnades and unadorned upper storeys: over the Marylebone Road, and there are more simple terraces, and finally, the glorious blocks of buildings—Chester Gate, Cumberland Terrace, Sussex Place, York Terrace—memorials to the greatest English town planning scheme yet put into practice. While behind Cumberland Terrace are, or rather were, smaller Regency streets—Cumberland Market, with the two-storey streets near it, 'workmen's dwellings' invented 100 years before their time.

And, where London led, the provinces followed.

The skill of Regency architects is best argued in their buildings. Before this book is remaindered there may still be a chance, the best chance I know, for Londoners of seeing how excellent the 'easy theatricalities of Nash' could be. Let the observer stand on the pavement outside Charing Cross Station. On his left there will be the last remaining stucco buildings in West Strand with a bank on their corner. Let him look at the treatment of that irregular corner, two circular towers engaged

to the building and neatly masking the awkward turn into the
street that runs alongside the east walls of St Martin-in-the-
Fields. Next let him look at the corner of the new South Africa
House by Sir Herbert Baker. Lyons, commercial to the last,
retain their ungainly shop front below; above, rises the blunt
nose of masonry, awkward, narrow, two-dimensional in
appearance, skimped in detail, ineffective in its half-hearted
effort at simplicity. The new South Africa House seems to be
the work of a timid man afraid of the importance of his site.
The corner opposite, though half the height of South Africa
House and as difficult a problem, is confident work. The buildings of the Regency need no praise; if only people will study
them, they speak for themselves. They are removed in this
muddled age because they do not speak loud enough. Here are
the masterpieces of the Regency and late Georgian architecture
in Great Britain. Look at them: Waterloo Bridge, all buildings
by Sir John Soane, Carlton House Terrace, Kensal Green, the
Screen at Hyde Park Corner, St Pancras Church, Regent's
Park, the National Gallery, Kennington, Stockwell, the Cus-
tom House, the British Museum, St Matthew's, Brixton, the
Soane Museum, the Dulwich Art Gallery, in London; St
George's Hall, Liverpool; the National Gallery, the High
School, most of the New Town in Edinburgh; the older parts
of the Necropolis, Glasgow; the late Nelson Pillar, Dublin; the
list is endless.

Up till now I have described the larger Regency schemes—
the monumental work, the churches and galleries and bridges
and terraces. There was another side to Regency architecture.

Perhaps it can be called a darker side. Growing industrialism required an architecture. Factories and warehouses needed architects, and from the Regency sprang an industrial architecture that was magnificent in its simplicity. Recently I visited Macclesfield. Of the housing in Macclesfield I know little, but I saw in those square blocks of factories, with their broad, oblong windows and pink bricks, cathedrals which were as imposing as the Protestant one in Liverpool. And of warehouses there are countless examples. Plain brick structures like those at St Katharine's Docks in London; so plain as to be 'modern', so useful as to be terrifying. The Regency was not afraid of the machine, for the machine was still under control. Factories were built worthy of the machine. Let no one think that the 'Industrial North' contains no architecture. Preston, Macclesfield, Hull, Bradford, the Potteries, and in fact even Leeds, are just as worthy of a visit for their factory architecture as are York and Durham for their cathedrals.

There was good reason for all this excellent architecture. It was the swan song of educated building. The industrialists were becoming rich, but they were as yet unterrified by their employees' threat

> *We'll not forget to pay the debt*
> *Incurred at Peterloo.*

and they threw in their lot with an aristocracy that was busy furthering the interests of Empire. With the money gained from growing capitalism and a Parliament unhampered by a Reform Bill, a genius of architecture like Nash would seize his

opportunity, flatter himself into a position, employ his willing
'ghosts' or hack-architects whose plans he signed, and rebuild
the earth. The change, more sudden and more dire in its
results than might have been expected, must be dealt with in
the next chapter. So far, the educated people were on top. These
were the last days of England and the best; she had created a
distinct 'Empire style', distinct from the French. Her simple
architecture was put up in all her colonies, in many of which it
has been allowed to remain. It is equally at home there as it is
in London; beloved of the Americans, not even despised in
Jamaica, the Regency architecture still stands for ubiquity and
restraint. British Government houses abroad had an austerity
and aloofness that matched the competent officials within
them. And if sometimes there was a bit of Mohammedan,
Gothic or Chinese decoration, what matter as yet? It was but
plaster deep, and behind was a solid British brick wall.

# Chapter VII · Middle Class Architecture

*The lady, married, found the house too small—*
*Two shabby parlours, and that ugly hall!*

Crabbe, *Tales of the Hall*, Book XVII

I said in my last chapter that an architectural sin in the Regency period was but plaster deep. There was a certain ostentation then, which, because it was not unsightly, need not be condemned. The Brighton Pavilion, which is now being carefully restored to its original Georgian splendour, is a case in point. Much that was bad originated thence; bamboo furniture, the extensive use of stained glass in the house, columns disguised as palm trees, elaborate fire-irons, frosted glass, an abundance of china ornaments. But in the Brighton Pavilion those objects were displayed with a tasteful abandon. George IV knew a good thing when he saw it. His architects—Nash, Repton and Porden—were men of sensibility. Brighton Pavilion is beautiful inside, even impressive. George IV was an aristocrat; his architects were learned in their art. And he was their patron.

So long as architecture remained in the hands of those that cared for it, no harm was done. Even the fashions could not affect it. A growing tendency to interior splendour at the expense of the exterior of a building, and an incipient Romanticism

that was started by Horace Walpole writing scandal from his
Gothick palace at Strawberry Hill, furthered by the mysterious doings of William Beckford in his miraculous Fonthill
Abbey, no doubt started the trouble. Sir Walter Scott, with
his antiquarianism as deep in its understanding of the mediaeval period as those little stucco Gothic houses ranged so neatly
in our English spas; Thomas Moore, with his 'Lalla Rookh'
and its drawing-room orientalism; Southey, with his decorative Eastern fancies; West and Haydon, with their 100 square
yard interpretations of history; even the imaginings of Keats
and Hood and Shelley, L. E. L. and Mrs Hemans may have
contributed to the misconception and over-romanticising of
domestic architecture that was let loose shortly after the
Reform Bill.

Fashionable authors may have started the idea of trouble, but
would-be fashionable people did the actual mischief. I am
reminded of Maria Edgeworth's *The Absentee* when Lady
Clonbrony, the wife of an obscure Irish peer, makes a dash at
entering London society by giving a rout. She must have the
newest decorations, so she hires Mr Soho, that man of taste, to
decorate her ball-room in the newest manner:

> The first architectural upholsterer of the age, as he styled
> himself, and was universally admitted to be by the world of
> fashion, then, with full powers given to him, spoke *en
> maitre. . . .*
>
> Of the value of a NAME no one could be more sensible
> than Mr Soho.

'Your la'ship sees—this is merely a scratch of my pencil—
Your la'ship's sensible—just to give you an idea of the shape,
the form of the thing—You fill up your angles here with
*encoinieres*—round your walls with the *Turkish tent drapery*—
a fancy of my own—in apricot cloth, or crimson velvet,
suppose, or, *en flute*, in crimson satin draperies, fanned and
riched with gold fringes, *en suite*—intermediate spaces,
Apollo's heads with gold rays—and here, ma'am, you place
four *chancelieres*, with chimeras at the corners, covered with
blue silk and silver fringe, elegantly fanciful—with my
STATIRA CANOPY here—light blue silk draperies—aerial
tint, with silver balls—and for seats here, the SERAGLIO
OTTOMANS, superfine scarlet—your paws—griffin—golden
—and golden tripods, here, with antique cranes—and oriental
alabaster tables here and there—quite appropriate, your
la-ship feels—

'And, let me reflect—For the next apartment, it strikes me
—as your la'ship don't value expense—*the Alhambra hangings*—my own thought entirely—Now, before I unroll them,
Lady Clonbrony, I must beg you'll not mention I've shown
them—I give you my sacred honour, not a soul has set eye
upon the Alhambra hangings, except Mrs Dareville, who
stole a peep—I refused, absolutely refused, the Duchess of
Torcaster—But I can't refuse your la'ship—So see, ma'am—
(unrolling them)—scagliola porphyry columns supporting
the grand dome—entablature, silvered and decorated with
imitation bronze ornaments—under the entablature, a
*valance in pelmets*, of puffed scarlet silk, would have an un-

paralleled effect, seen through the arches—with the TRE-
BISOND TRELLICE PAPER, would make a *tout ensemble*,
novel beyond example—On that Trebisond trellice paper, I
confess, ladies, I do pique myself—

'Then for the little room, I recommend turning it temporarily into a Chinese pagoda with this *Chinese pagoda
paper*, with the *porcelain border*, and josses, and jars, and
beakers, to match; and I can venture to promise one vase of
pre-eminent size and beauty—O, indubitably! if your la'ship
prefers it, you can have the *Egyptian hieroglyphic paper*, with
the *ibis border*, to match!—The only objection is, one sees it
everywhere—quite antediluvian—gone to the hotels even—
But, to be sure, if you la'ship has a fancy—At all events, I
humbly recommend, what his Grace of Torcaster longs to
patronise, my MOON CURTAINS, with candlelight draperies
—A demisaison elegance this—I hit off yesterday—and—
True, your la'ship's quite correct—out of the common, com-
pletely—And, of course, you'd have the *sphynx candelabras*,
and the Phoenix argands—O! nothing else lights now, ma'am
—Expense!—Expense of the whole!—Impossible to calcu-
late here on the spot!—But nothing at all worth your lady-
ship's consideration!—'

But alas for Lady Clonbrony! Both Mrs Dareville and the
Duchess, when they swept in late and went away early from
the poor lady's party, made mock of her decorations. The true
aristocracy still had its standards of art. But it is interesting to
see that as early as 1812, when this novel was written, money

could be made out of the uneducated rich. And if in 1812 so much money could be made—how much more in 1872, when Sir Georgius Midas had made his little packet; when cotton, railways, iron, cement, gas companies, telegraph companies, steamships, and the thousand methods of mass production in trades unheard of in 1812, had made their appearance and brought with them the wealth which prevented the sun from ever setting, except on domestic architecture, when it seemed to have set for ever. As yet there was a childish delight in the sight of approaching industry. The great Tennyson himself regarded it with a playful patronage in 'The Princess':

> strange was the sight to me ;
> For all the sloping pasture murmur'd, sown
> With happy faces and with holiday
> There moved the multitude, a thousand heads :
> The patient leaders of their Institute
> Taught them with facts. One rear'd a font of stone
> And drew, from butts of water on the slope,
> The fountain of the moment, playing now
> A twisted snake, and now a rain of pearls,
> Or steep-up spout, whereon the gilded ball
> Danced like a wisp : and somewhat lower down
> A man with knobs and wires and vials fired
> A canon. Echo answer'd in her sleep
> From hollow fields : and here were telescopes
> For azure views ; and there a group of girls
> In circle waited, whom the electric shock

*Dislink'd with shrieks and laughter : round the lake*
*A little clock-work steamer paddling plied*
*And shook the lilies : perch'd about the knolls*
*A dozen angry models jetted steam :*
*A petty railway van : a fire-balloon*
*Rose gem-like up before the dusky groves*
*And dropt a fairy parachute and past :*
*And there through twenty posts of telegraph*
*They flash'd a saucy message to and fro*
*Between the mimic stations ; so that sport*
*Went hand in hand with Science : . . .*

No, it is not on the Gothic revival that much-abused, if some-what self-conscious effort to set things aright, that the blame can be laid; nor is it on the improved methods of transport; for travel did no harm to those who made the Grand Tour in the eighteenth century. The cause for the over-romanticising of domestic and civic architecture in the nineteenth century was the wealth of the nineteenth century. Although the Reform Bill of 1832 may have made little difference in the matter of actual class distinctions at the time, not giving at once the Parliamentary power to the capitalist that he needed, it was the first wise step of stealth. Cooper describes the capitalist in 'The Purgatory of Suicides' in 1845:

             *ever of power appearing coy,*
    *Continuing antique symbols to employ,—*
    *Titles and forms of the old Commonwealth,—*

*Hallowing the shade securely to destroy*
*The substance of licentiousness : wise stealth*
*By which the pulse of sovereignty gained vigorous health.*

The merchant prince, the manufacturer who had built that fine stucco mansion, was willing to allow the aristocracy some substance of power while it suited his ends. That he was conscious of his own power is obvious enough. You will remember Miss Dunstable, the heiress whose father had made a fortune in ointment, in Trollope's novel, *Dr. Thorne* (1858). She is talking to Mr Moffat, the rich son of a tailor, where they are staying in Lord de Courcy's house:

'It is a strange thing, is it not,' said he [Mr. Moffat] recurring to his old view of the same subject, 'that I should be going to dine with the Duke of Omnium—the richest man, they say, among the whole English aristocracy?'

'Men of that kind entertain everybody, I believe, now and then,' said Miss Dunstable, not very civilly.

'I believe they do; but I am not going as one of the everybodies. I am going from Lord de Courcy's house with some of his own family. . . . Yes; wealth is very powerful: here we are, Miss Dunstable, the most honoured guests in this house. . . . It is quite delightful to watch these people, now they accuse us of being tuft hunters.'

'Do they?' said Miss Dunstable. 'Upon my word, I didn't know that anybody ever so accused me.'

'I didn't mean you and me personally.'

'Oh, I'm glad of that.'

'But that is what the world says of persons of our class. Now it seems to me that the toadying is all on the other side. The countess here does toady you, and so do the young ladies.'

And so we watch the new aristocracy leavening the old.

The aristocracy of industry or education does not alter the course of architecture, though indirectly it may affect it. Mr Moffat and Miss Dunstable will possess houses, heavy, indeed, with their furniture, ostentatious perhaps in their efforts in decoration to get away from former styles. No, the chief cutter in Mr Moffat's tailoring establishment is comparatively rich now, the foremen in Miss Dunstable's inherited ointment factory want more sumptuous dwellings than those hurriedly erected alongside the factory to house a growing population— erected there, to save money and time in transport.

And those foremen and cutters, the grocer and the haber- dasher regain something that will show they are a station above the mere manual workers in the factory and assistants in the shop. A farcical replica of a feudal house is reproduced. Instead of forty rooms, there are four or six. But those are crowded with all the devices imitating wealth that increasing mass pro- duction can supply. Bamboo furniture, insecure replicas of work in His Majesty's Pavilion at Brighton, an harmonium in place of the organ in the grand hall, a terra-cotta ridge tile in place of the stone gargoyle on the ancestral mansion, an Ax- minster in place of a Persian rug; vegetation in the parlour, since there is insufficient area for a greenhouse. And those neat exteriors, those rows of dwellings spaciously arranged, two storeys high and rarely displaying anything but the most elegant freak of decoration, became coarsened. The architraves of the windows assumed an Italian air, the hall ceiling attempted to imitate the work of Wren; so did the plaster moulding on the outside of the neighbouring public-house. For Londoners the whole area containing that style of architecture is embraced by the old North London Railway which, until the war, ran no trains during church time on Sundays. It runs from Broad Street to Richmond, and traverses Canonbury, Dalston, Mildmay Park, Highbury, Camden Town, Kentish Town, Gospel Oak, Hampstead Heath, Finchley Road, Brondesbury, Kensal Rise, Willesden, Acton, Kew and Richmond, districts which contain every phase of Victorian architecture from the Italianate stucco of Dalston and Hackney to the red brick Flemish revival of Brondesbury and the Venetian Gothic of Kew.

And in grander quarters the same coarsening of architecture went on. I choose London for examples of the styles, because I know London. South Kensington and Pimlico, those long streets with rows of Tuscan porticoes, dark basements, wet, arid squares, where

*I am aware of the damp souls of housemaids*
*Sprouting despondently at area gates,*

those houses in what Mr Clough Williams-Ellis calls the Pimlico Palladian style, and where he says one feels that the architect had one sense lacking, that he was, perhaps, deaf.

Nor was the Gothic Revival of the early and mid-Victorian periods particularly successful. Imitations of the unconscious eccentricities of the mediaeval period, in cast iron or patent stone, unnecessary roughening of the surface of stone, prickly spires and chemical stained glass windows produced a travesty of Middle Ages successful on the surface only: what Mr Alan Pryce Jones describes as a literary interpretation of the past as literary as the Tractarian movement. Who does not know, as he gazes from some hotel or boarding-house window, that inevitable Gothic spire, prickly and mis-shapen, pricking the skyline above the smoky housetops? And who does not realise the full significance of remarks like these in Kelly's Directories:

LOATHLY-CRUMPET WITH MUCKBY, four miles east of Horncastle in the County of Lincolnshire. The living is a rectory, the joint gift of the Pastoral Aid Society and the Bishop of Norwich, and has been held since 1871 by the Reverend Wesley Emmanuel Camp, B.A., of Durham University. The net income is £108 per annum, including glebe and parsonage. The church of St Botolph is an ancient building in stone and flint consisting of nave, chancel, two aisles and an embattled western tower. In 1864 the church was thoroughly restored under the supervision of Gilbert Scott, when the nave was reseated in pitch-pine and a new chancel added in the Decorated Gothic style. In 1880 a further restoration took place, when a new vestry was added and the old organ removed from the west gallery and a fine new one added to the chancel. The floor was also relaid with encaustic tiles. In 1900 the windows were filled with stained glass, depicting Faith, Hope, Charity, Evangelisation, mission work in Africa and kindred subjects, through the generosity of Miss Loathly, of Loathly Hall. The war memorial is in a stained-glass west window. Muckby Church whose living is held jointly with Loathly-Crumpet, yielding £18 a year, is a modern erection built in a pseudo-Italian style in 1764. It is used now only as a mortuary chapel. The chief landowner is Miss Mary Pamela Camilla Loathly, whose mansion, Loathly Hall, erected from the designs of Mr Evan Christian in 1872, is situated in this parish.

Glorious Lincolnshire, where—except for the Edwardian gaiety of Woodhall Spa, that half-timbered Camberley among unexpected fir trees—the Victorian life goes on, unhampered by a convenient railway system and not 'picturesque' enough for the main-road motorist.

Here is a poem describing a Victorian church:

*The Church's restoration*
*  In 1883*
*Has left for contemplation*
*  Not what there used to be.*
*How well the ancient woodwork*
*  Looks round the Rect'ry hall,*
*Memorial of the good work*
*  Of him who plann'd it all.*

*He who took down the pew ends*
*  And sold them anywhere,*
*But kindly spared a few ends*
*  Worked up into a chair;*

*Oh worthy persecution*
  *Of dust ; oh hue divine !*
*Oh cheerful substitution*
  *Thou varnishéd pitch-pine !*

*Church furnishing ! Church furnishing !*
  *Come Mowbray swell the praise.\**
*He gave the brass for burnishing,*
  *He gave the thick red baize ;*
*He gave the new addition*
  *Pull'd down the dull old aisle,*
*To pave the sweet transition,*
  *He gave th' encaustic tile !*

*Of marble brown and veinéd*
  *He did the pulpit make,*
*He order'd windows stainéd*
  *Light red and crimson lake.*
*Sing on with hymns uproarious*
  *Ye humble and aloof !*
*Look up—and oh ! how glorious !*
  *He has restored the roof !*

But it is tiresome to laugh at Victorian solecisms. It has been
done too often. For those who wish to read a far from laughable

* Mowbrays at the time objected to their name being used, because they thought
it detrimental to their church-furnishing business. I was sent for to see them in
their Margaret Street shop. The edition was withdrawn, the page was cancelled,
and a feebler line with no names in it substituted.

study of the earlier part of the Gothic revival, I can recommend Mr Kenneth Clark's book on that subject.

The true English tradition of national craftsmanship never died in the Victorian era. That is a superficial criticism, often aimed at an age of mass production and but partially organised industrialism.

Perhaps it were well to take the good craftsmanship in Victorian domestic architecture first. I admit willingly that it did not reside with architects, and but rarely with builders. Speculation in houses saw to that. In the house, however, woman, aware of her place, that of doing crochetwork, embroidery, shell work, painting, dressmaking while waiting for baby, produced exquisitely-made articles that are the pride of families whose ancestors go back to Victorian times.

But by far the finest tradition of architecture set by the Victorian age was in her commercial enterprises. We do not realise today the courage required to build a railway to the North of England, a house of glass like the Crystal Palace, a development scheme like that extending from the Albert Memorial to the Museum district of South Kensington. It is in these schemes that the great English architectural tradition was ahead of Europe. Whoever considers King's Cross Station today? Yet it is one of the finest buildings in the world. Two enormous brick arches filled with glass, divided by a plain tower with no superfluous decoration. The offices, blocks, and the crescent-shaped hotel form part of the same scheme, simple buildings with an appropriate veneer of classical decoration. And inside the station are those two great receding tunnels of glass, with their rhythmical pattern of iron girders and supports.

Next door is St Pancras Station, with its fantastic Gothic hotel, before which Sir Gilbert Scott, the architect, is said to have exclaimed, 'It is too beautiful!' Behind it is one of the largest roofs of a single span in the world. More beautiful though no less daring than the hotel. The hotel reminds me of a pompous alderman with an enormous watch-chain, flaring tie and pearl tiepin masking a bosom in which beats a worthy heart.

Nor are railways, with their handsome locomotives, the only examples of England's innate architectural sense. In the countless factories, unadorned workplaces of the North, in machines, in engine sheds, in cast-iron bridges, in the work of railway and bridge engineers, even in gasometers, the English tradition was carried on, albeit unconsciously.

Only when 'architecture' was considered something to stick on to a building afterwards to make it 'showy' or upper class, were the mistakes made. Heaven knows there were hundreds of such mistakes. But they were good, vulgar mistakes, like a dropped 'h'. I would any day prefer an ornate sham-marble Victorian mantel to a 'refeened' pseudo-Queen Anne effort designed by some pupil of an architectural school today.

Victorian architecture exactly reflected the middle class, the backbone of England, which industrialism had created. In its utilitarian buildings it was honest and often imaginative, in its domestic buildings naïvely snobbish, as unpleasant but as well intended, as grocer's port. The 'refeenment' and 'good taste' which killed English architecture, at any rate, as a national style, must wait until the next chapter.

# Chapter VIII · Revolt in the Middle Classes

*Refinement and Refeenment*
*Good Taste*

*The isles saw it and feared.*—Isaiah xliv

In 1874 the new Law Courts were begun. Little more than a decade before, the flagstaff had been erected on the Victoria Tower of the Houses of Parliament after the last stone had been laid. Street built the Law Courts, and Barry built the Houses of Parliament. And in those two buildings lies the whole history of great Victorian architecture. The era which had started so well with Barry's stupendous achievement, the Houses of Parliament, ended in that colossal failure, the new Law Courts, which guards Fleet Street still, like some fossilised, but none the less impressive, brontosaurus. And perhaps it is by contrasting the careers of Sir Charles Barry and George Edmund Street that we may see how architecture has become so diverse today. For Barry was in the old architectural tradition—self-educated, a demon for work, an artist and a visionary. Street was in the new tradition, a gentleman, well educated, a scholar, an artist and a visionary. Barry was unself-conscious, Street the reverse. Barry allowed his scholarship to be no more than his slave. He tamed Italian palaces into London clubs, and

Henry VII's Chapel into the Houses of Parliament; only here
and there did he make a mistake. Street always considered his
scholarship first, and let his own ideas work themselves out
within the limits allowed by a somewhat pedantic conscience.
He never tamed anything. He died beaten by his own master,
the Gothic Revival, when fierce contentions rated over his
beloved Law Courts. And there they stand today, dated and
dead, while Barry's masterpiece is as alive as ever.

The Law Courts were the death knell of the old-fashioned
scholarly Gothic. Obviously something was wrong with them.
They were like a cathedral, certainly, but somehow they
needed monks and priests and bishops.

And as much as the Gothic Revival had become a self-
conscious and a moral affair, the classical architecture which
had glorified the Regency period lost its vigour in these fierce
commercial times. I have shown in another chapter how the
districts of Pimlico and South Kensington are unwieldy
memorials of its downfall. Classical architecture became Italianate and attenuated, in its effort to keep pace with the Gothic
Revival, and in Edward Middleton Barry's Cannon Street
Hotel we see a similar effort to St Pancras carried out in the
classical manner.

All such monumental architecture of public buildings and
the larger merchants' mansions had become the work of architects who were ruined by self-consciousness, who were horrified
lest they should betray some false scholarship by building any
large edifice in a straightforward way.

Domestic architecture had come to a pretty pass. The rapidly

increasing population requiring small houses were swindled by
speculators almost as much as they are swindled by them today.
Houses were built by visionaries, or else by speculative speculators in land, in stained glass for front doors, in cast iron rail-
ings, in terra-cotta ridge tiles, in mosaic pavements for front
gardens, in bamboo furniture, in mahogany sideboards, in
Japanese fans, in horsehair coverings, in moulded classical cornices, in marble and imitation marble mantels, in vases, in
bowls, in coloured tiles, in coloured door knobs, in wallpaper,
flowered and classical, in capitals, Gothic and Romanesque;
in window-boxes, sashes, frosted or stained glass, glazing bars;
in brass knobs for bedsteads, in brass bedsteads for knobs, in
the thousands of superfluities which make a home a home and a
house different from its neighbour alongside it, and to all but
its owner a just estimate of an income of its inmate. The
suburbs of every manufacturing town, the pretentious villa in
a village trying to look like a bit of East Ham in Melbury
Bubb; every front door imitating the window of a parish
church, every name in glass above it lit by a flaming gas jet
behind, picked out in flamboyant lettering and recalling the
name of one of the stately homes of England, although the
number is 37 and more convenient for the post office; these are
the products of speculating building.

It is, therefore, hardly surprising that those middle-class
Victorians, whose eyes were not blinded by the dust from the
progressive march of industrialism, should have attempted
to have a little aesthetic revolution on their own. It was a
revolution which had disastrous effects, as we shall see later;

it was the revolution of 'back to mediaevalism' in the face of
Sir Gilbert Scott and G. E. Street. Gothic practised by the
pundits was not mediaeval enough. William Morris and the
pre-Raphaelite brotherhood escaped from the din and the roar
of commerce. They escaped to those flat meadows of Lechlade,
where Kelmscot Manor still stands among the elms, and
where Miss May Morris still waves from her father's bold
designs. But as she and hundreds of others influenced by the
Morris movement weave and weave with lily hands the trailing
beautiful patterns of their inspirer, patterns equally good in a
different way are stamped, edged and spun by machines, are
made faster and faster, until the fingers of the gentlefolk
weavers tire and fall into their home-spun laps. It is easy
enough to laugh at the Morris movement. It was as scholarly
as architecture practised by architects had become, but it was
a domestic movement. Besides Philip Webb, there was no
great early interpreter of Morris in brick and stone; they
were to come later.

Morris came like a healthy breeze, pleading his doctrine of
escape in an impossible guild socialism capable of succeeding
only in remote agricultural villages.

> From township to township, o'er down and by tillage
> Far, far have we wander'd and long was the day,
> But now cometh eve at the end of the village
> Where over the grey wall the church riseth grey.
>
> There is wind in the twilight; in the white road before us
> The straw from the ox yard is blowing about,

*The moon's rim is rising, a dove glitters o'er us*
*And the vane on the spire top is swinging in doubt.*

*Down there dips the highway, toward the bridge crossing over*
*The brook that runs on to the Thames and the sea,*
*[Draw closer my sweet, we are lover and lover,*
*This eve thou art given to gladness and me.]*

What a blessed relief from New Cross and Hornsey, from Pimlico and Manchester, but how impossible and how cowardly an escape!

We have made the machines and there they are. We have let them get the better of us. The pure doctrines of Morris certainly purified English architecture, though they only purified domestic architecture. The work of Charles Francis Annesley Voysey, a master of all crafts, which carried on and made known to the Continent that architecture was still alive in England, was perhaps the finest flowering of actual self-conscious architecture in Victorian England. We all know the sort of houses he built and those his imitators built. They are situated generally in Buckinghamshire. Steep and broad-slated roofs with tapering chimneys are supported by thin walls heavily buttressed. The windows, high under the roof and again near the ground, are long and low. Inside, the furniture is simple and hand-made of unstained oak, probably pierced with hearts. The walls are whitewashed, and the chintzes are designed in bright primary colours. There is an atmosphere of health, of the windows flung open, of bright nurseries and clean bathrooms, of the smell of soap, of wholemeal bread, of vegetarianism,

Quakerism and sober gaiety that marks the beginning of emancipation in the early twentieth century. Sir Edwin Lutyens started as a follower of Voysey when he built his beautiful smaller houses; Guy Dawber and Baillie Scott followed close behind. A prophet is not without honour . . . Voysey lives today. Of such stuff as these houses were made garden cities, our most important contribution to the all-important subject of town planning.

Influenced by Voysey, and reacting from the sham classicalism of Norman Shaw,* came the Art Nouveau movement of 1900. It was the longest stride in the right direction. It looked to find new forms, and discarded the old shibboleths of crockets or classical orders. It died a quick death. Its greatest exponent was characteristically a Scotsman, Charles Rennie Mackintosh, who died almost forgotten in 1924. He may be said to have founded 'modern' architecture as it is to be seen in Germany. He had no fear of blank surfaces, and made windows only where he needed them. His finest work is the Glasgow Art School. We would have none of his work in England, but until the war simple contemporary architecture, such as that practised by that master genius, Peter Behrens, was known in Germany as *Mackintoshismus*.

The lily roots and twisted horrors of Art Nouveau had been straightened out, and the simple architecture goes on today with the work, among others, of practical men like Frederick Etchells, Wells Coates, Joseph Emberton and a few others.

There were, indeed, disastrous results of this domestic

* Who, I now realise, was our greatest architect since Wren, if not greater.

Morris movement of architecture, but not so disastrous as those of a classical revival specially suited to 'educated' architects, who liked to show off their knowledge of Renaissance detail—a novel knowledge in 1880—and whose leader was Norman Shaw. Of this gentleman's work the less said the better. He was a facile, expensive and pretentious architect, who, like many of his followers, had a facility for catching rich clients.

Except for the fine streak in domestic architecture which I have mentioned, building ceased to be of anything but commercial importance in England after 1860. For those who have a taste for the morbid I have appended a genealogical tree (pp. 108–9)—perforce, rather too sweeping—showing the results and reactions of self-conscious stylism.

# THE GROWTH
## OF
## 'GOOD TASTE'

THE GROWT

VICTO

*The Law Courts, Lon*
*Doulton's Factories; Got.*

MAINLY
DOMESTIC

NOTE.—Buildings and architects shown in
heavy type in this genealogy represent the thin
stream of life and vigorous influence for the
good in English architecture for the last fifty
years. The italics represent stagnant architecture, which is a dead end in itself, being lost in
self-conscious efforts either to parade 'scholarship' or 'value for money' or else to make an
ineffectual 'tasteful' compromise between the
new and the old.

PRE-RAPHAELITES AND WILLIAM MORRIS
*living in the Cotswolds and doing everything by hand under guild socialism; domesticity.*

TUDOR REVIVALS
Pusey House, Oxford; St Cyprian's Church,
Clarence Gate, London;
*Liverpool Cathedral; The Scottish War Memorial;*
the work of Comper and Temple Moore.

SIMPLE DOMESTIC
ARCHITECTURE
The houses of Voysey, Lutyens, Baillie Sc
and Dawber; health and unstained oak f
niture.

*Arts and Crafts. Gentle folk*
*weaving and spinning;*
*Modern Church Furnishing;*
*Olde Teae Shoppes.*

*Sham Tudor Revival. Most*
*modern roadside public-*
*houses; Clifton Court,*
*Maida Vale, London; all*
*'architect-designed' Tudor*
*residences.*

GARDEN CITIES
Hampstead, Bourn-
ville, Welwyn, Letch-
worth, Port Sunlight.
Sir Raymond Unwin.

ART NOUVEAU
This was possibly an
illegitimate child of
above. Slater's; Old
Underground Statio
London; Metro en-
trances; Horniman
Museum, London.

C. R. MACKINTO
Glasgow Art School.

Crawford's Building, Holborn, London; Yacht Club,
Burnham-on-Crouch; Cresta Shops, London;
Olympia; Baptist Church, East Barnet, Herts;
Engine Rooms *of large pseudo-classical offices.*

THE DEEP PIT OF

OOD TASTE'

CTURE

'ermini of England;
d over-restored Churches.

MAINLY
PUBLIC

i-mediaeval reaction under Norman Shaw. Piccadilly Hotel, London; Fitzjohn's Avenue, London; Royal
graphical Society, London (not modern part); Clouds, Wiltshire.

| | |
|---|---|
| e Flemish and Jacobean Revival. Imperial Hotel, London; mination Schools, Oxford; countless examples in a cotta and brick; Pont Street, London; all tral Manchester; Palace Theatre, London. | Unrestrained Classical. Imperial Institute; Central Hall, Westminster; Ritz Hotel, London; Belfast Town Hall; Admiralty New Buildings; almost all twentieth century town halls, public libraries and lavatories and fire stations and police courts; White City; Earl's Court, London; interior decorators' Mayfair-Italianate; Ecclesiastical-Spanish; 'Victorian'. |

trained 'Renaissance', practised by most members of the R.I.B.A. 'Good
te'. The New Regent Street; South Africa House; Lambeth Bridge;
imes House; Unilever House; Wembley; the proposed (and pray God rejected)
n for Carlton House Terrace.

'Restrained', 'Modern' and pseudo-Swedish;
Architectural Association average student's work.

z, Modern. Artillery House, London; Adelaide
use, London; pseudo-modern factories with Egyptian
ives; all cheap cushions and fabrics and handbags and
rays and teacups, which depend on strident colours
hed together for their effect; most new cinemas.

LATIVE BUILDING

# Conclusion

*And the parched ground shall become a pool, and the thirsty land springs of water: in the habitation of dragons, where each lay, shall be grass with reeds and rushes.*—Isaiah xxxv. 7

And now what of the future? I have taken a clean sheet of paper because I do not wish to hamper my mind with the thoughts that surge up in me at the sight of Mr Peter Fleetwood-Hesketh's devilish drawings, or of the art in Shaftesbury Avenue or the new Regent Street.

Architects today ought to be the most important men in the country.

Nearly all the suburbs and centres of towns are badly planned. An architect must be a town planner.

Steel, concrete, glass and plywood have made a new era in building. New proportions and new masses and new systems of heating, lighting and ventilation have been called into being. Only 100 years ago a water-closet was unheard of. An architect must be every sort of engineer.

There are more swindlers about than ever there were in the eighteenth century. An architect must be a business man.

Where has English architectural talent disappeared? Native ability to design is alive. No other country than our own can make such beautiful motor cars, railway locomotives, buses or trams. English craftsmen can be competent and thorough as many British workmen. The housewives' dream, the labour-saving kitchen, that throbbing heart of efficiency in the midst of the dead 'period' decoration of every villa in lovely Mill Hill, Hendon Heights, healthy Edgware, bracing Bootle, beechy Bucks, charming Surrey or moderate Morden contains all the architectural ingenuity required to plan a town.

Architecture is not dead, it needs co-ordination.

Who is to co-ordinate so many talents? The genius is there, though I doubt whether all the knowledge required for an architect today could be co-ordinated in one man. We have created a specialised civilisation, so that its architecture will require specialised departments. In a system of commercial competition this is impossible. So far we have had to be content with the pseudo-Renaissance efforts of a be-knighted archi-tecture—architecture as affected and 'naice' as a refeened accent and hardly preferable to the dropped 'h's' of a specula-tive builder.

And this is where I clinch the argument by which I have attempted to hold together this book. Since architecture is too big a job for one man, several men must do it. This will never be done under a system which allows the 'gentlemen' to show off their knowledge of period, while the all-important engineers have their good work hidden by these self-conscious marks.

Several men, each working in his own department, can be made harmonious by a unity of ideals, as men worked in Regency or mediaeval days. This is obvious enough. We have seen in this book how English architecture emerged from the religious unity of Christendom to the reasoned unity of an educated monarchic system, and then to the stranger order of an industralised community. As soon as it became unsettled, towards the end of the nineteenth century, 'architecture' *qua* architecture became self-conscious. Only in trades which were alive and prosperous did good design continue. Now those trades are declining and architecture is no less self-conscious.

Architecture can only be made alive again by a new order and another Christendom. I repeat that I do not know what form that Christendom will take, for I am not an economist. It is unlikely that it will be capitalism. Whatever it is, this generation will not see it.

*Castlepollard—Capri—Heston-Hounslow—Wiesbaden.*